The Book of Famous Oddballs

Did you know that

Dr Johnson was amazingly strong? When he found a man sitting in his seat at the theatre, and the interloper refused to budge, he picked up man and chair and hurled them into the pit.

Casanova used to grow the nail on his little finger extra long so that he could pick the wax out of his ears with it?

George Washington's false teeth were made from the tusks of a hippopotamus?

And much, much more?

The Book of Famous Oddballs

Dave Dutton

ARROW BOOKS

Arrow Books Limited
62–65 Chandos Place, London WC2N 4NW

An imprint of Century Hutchinson Ltd

London Melbourne Sydney Auckland
Johannesburg and agencies throughout
the world

First published 1986

Photoset by Rowland Phototypesetting Limited
Bury St Edmunds, Suffolk
Printed and bound in Great Britain by
Anchor Brendon Limited, Tiptree, Essex

ISBN 0 09 943250 1

Contents

Foreword

They are shot at, spat at, slandered, preyed upon by cadgers and thieves; punched, poked, prodded, pawed and pestered in public; hounded, told lies about, live in fear of having their offspring kidnapped; are the subject of envy and jealousy; have eggs thrown at them; are accosted frequently by people they've never seen before; have their private lives paraded in the newspapers; get asked to open church bazaars and have people they'd rather forget fling their arms round them and tell embarrassing tales about them on 'This Is Your Life'. Who are these poor beleaguered individuals?

The famous

What is fame? 'The advantage of being known by people of whom you yourself know nothing and *care* even less', said Stanislas Leszinski. Who he? King of Poland who lived from 1677 to 1766 (see, you've forgotten him already). Harassed on all sides, yet striving for a wider affection, some go through all manner of hell and humiliation to achieve that state known as being famous. Some would even *kill* for that dubious honour. In the wake of the assassination attempt on President Reagan and the tragic gunning-down of John Lennon, people took to wearing tee-shirts with the impassioned plea 'DON'T SHOOT ME – I'M NOT FAMOUS'. Incidentally, if you think that shooting a head of state to gain fame is a modern phenomenon, it's not – a twenty-year-old Saxon by the name of Von der Sulhn was arrested in Paris and confessed that it was his intention to kill Napoleon – thus immortalizing his own name by linking it forever with that of the illustrious French emperor. The fact that they are too pathetic to become famous by more creative or worthier schemes seems to escape them. They end up as objects of scorn and derision.

Once achieved, what is this fame? 'Men's fame is like their hair which grows after they are dead – and with just as little use to them', opined George Villiers, second Duke of Buckingham (1628–1687). Surely you've heard of *him*?

For Alexander Pope, and other successful poets before and after I should imagine, it meant mounds of poems sent to his home by hundreds of poetasters seeking his advice. It drove him to distraction – as did the unwanted manuscripts received by Sir Walter Scott (see text) who was plagued by rubbernecking sightseers, including stacks of American tourists, at his home. On one day alone no less than *sixteen* parties of visitors asked to be shown round his house. Even Wordsworth had a constant flow of uninvited pests at his Rydal Mount home. No wonder he did most of his composing *al fresco* (also see text). When asked by a visitor to be shown to Wordsworth's study, a servant took him to the library and said: 'This is the master's library – but he *studies* in the fields . . .'

Oh yes, it's all very well being famous for them as wants to be, but how many of us would like, when we die, to have hairs snatched from our beards as souvenirs or be used as a salt-cellar, as befell one poor soul in this book?

Within the covers of this book, I guarantee that you will find some amazing, amusing and shocking facts about famous folk – facts your history teacher never taught you.

I've sleuthed beneath the public façade to find out what the golden lads and lasses were *really* like – their bizarre behaviour, their tastes in sex, their oddball habits and their strange little ways. For instance, Tennyson's poems I can take or leave but the fact that he used to do impressions of a man on the lavatory fascinates me, both in the imagery that it conjures up in my mind's eye and the little insight it provides into Tennyson's lighter side.

You too need never be stuck for an answer in conversational one-upmanship. You may not know a great deal about the social and national ramifications of the English Civil War, but I guarantee you'll knock 'em dead when you sally forth with: 'Ah yes, but did you know that Charles the First had *rickets* . . .?'

I've had a lot of fun researching this book, and I hope that you will have as much fun in reading it and finding out about the little frailties and foibles of the famous.

Henry Thoreau said that 'Our admiration of a famous man lessens upon our nearer acquaintance with him; and we seldom hear of a celebrated person without a catalogue of some of his weaknesses and infirmities.'

This could be the catalogue he was talking about. Dip into it and laugh . . . but before you laugh *too* loudly, just ask yourself this: would you like *your* little imperfections and idiosyncracies made known to a wider public?

No? Then the chances are that if they aren't, it's only because *you're not famous* . . .

Dave Dutton

Twenty Questions

How much do you know about famous people? Here is a questionnaire relating to the famous folk in this book. You shouldn't know the answers to more than a couple of them. If you do, congratulations . . . you have a laudatory taste for the uncommon.

PS The answers are at the back – but don't look until you've read the book.

1 Who shocked Queen Victoria by jumping out from under a table in the nude?

2 Which English king was used as a salt-cellar?

3 Which so-called sex expert married a lesbian?

4 Which famous British prime minister had Red Indian blood in his veins and wore pink silk underwear?

5 Who was the king who discussed politics with a tree?

6 What sad end did Judy Garland have in common with King George II?

7 Which Roman ruler brought out a law sanctioning farting at the dinner table?

8 Who was the French wit who ate the contents of his chamber-pot?

9   Which famous English queen was a flasher?

10   Which great French emperor had his penis stolen?

11   Which romantic poet thought he had elephantiasis?

12   Which eminent Victorian artist tried to suffocate an old woman by sitting on her chest?

13   Which famous English poet had sex with a monkey – then ate it?

14   Which American president is now an angel in the Vatican?

15   Which famous explorer died of piles?

16   Who was the German ruler who bit his uncles' legs?

17   Which author of one of the world's most famous children's stories enjoyed taking photographs of young naked girls as his hobby?

18   Which British prime minister whipped himself before and after visiting brothels?

19   Which British monarch had his wife's lover murdered and stuffed under her floorboards?

20   Which birth control pioneer thought all men should wear kilts and didn't know what masturbation was until she was twenty-nine?

1
Boets and Bainters (and Penmen in General)

Wherein we meet . . . Dylan the dog . . . Charles Kingsley and his postponed honeymoon . . . Dr Johnson under the lash . . . Wordsworth sans teeth . . . Swinburne and his monkey lover . . . Mrs Whistler's son . . . Tennyson and his odd impersonations . . . Voltaire's shocking repast . . . and so to bed with Sam Pepys – and what he got up to while he was there.

'I hate *all* Boets and Bainters.' *King George I of England*

Dylan Thomas, *Welsh poet*

. . . was frequently to be found crawling around on his hands and knees, barking loudly – under the impression that he was a dog. Once, claiming he'd got rabies, he terrorized a crowded hotel with his canine capers, which ended when he scampered outside and chipped a tooth while biting a lamp-post. He performed the same doggy

13

antics in public houses, often biting people on the legs and bottom.

In America for a lecture tour, a woman who asked him to read to her from a book of his poems screamed when he promptly dropped to his knees and stuck his head up her skirt.

At Cambridge University, he was once seen doing his impression of a dog under a table and was kept happy by the occasional pat on the head.

His imagination tended towards the bizarre. He often wondered what it would be like to eat a dried eyeball sandwich or one with a filling of honey and mouse.

He contemplated what it would feel like to lie naked in a bath while white mice crawled all over him.

The first poem that he ever sold to a newspaper – 'His Requiem' – wasn't written by him at all even though he had claimed the authorship. He had copied it from a comic – *The Boys' Own Paper* – and sent it off in his name. The plagiarism only came to light in 1971 when *The Sunday Times* published it as Thomas's and an eagle-eyed reader pointed out that it had in fact been written by a lady named Lillian Gard, who specialized in writing for children's magazines.

Charles Kingsley, *The Water Babies author and Queen Victoria's chaplain*

. . . was a theologian, canon of Westminster and a racist. He described blacks as 'ant-eating apes' and Irishmen as 'white chimpanzees'. He also felt that the wrong side had won the American Civil War.

A visit to a prostitute while a student seems to have filled him with long-lasting feelings of guilt about sex. While working as a curate in Hampshire, he was separated from his bride-to-be, Fanny. In penitence for impure thoughts

14

he went into a wood, took off all his clothes and lay naked on a bed of thorns – which tore his flesh from head to foot. He also fasted and slept on the floor.

He asked Fanny to refrain from intercourse for a month after they were married in 1844 on the basis that by so doing, they would be giving their lovemaking such sanctity that they would be able to make love without interruption when they eventually reached Heaven.

Instead of making love, they learned German. Their daughter, Rose Georgiana, was born *ten months exactly* after the wedding.

For his book on Saint Elizabeth of Hungary, he drew his own illustrations, which consisted mainly of nude women being tortured.

He suffered from a very bad stammer.

He thought that blood sports should be encouraged and that killing animals was 'delightful'.

Honoré de Balzac, *French novelist*

. . . was a short, fat glutton. Once, at a single sitting, he ate 100 oysters, 12 cutlets, 2 partridges, a duck, a sole, 12 pears and several puddings for good measure.

Lewis Carroll, *author*

. . . was obsessed with little girls and enjoyed taking photographs of them with no clothes on (the girls, that is). The artist E. Gertrude Thomson, who used naked child models, provided him with the children who posed in the nude for him. Most were below the age of puberty.

On returning from his holidays, he always made a careful note of all the young girls he had met there.

His most famous book was originally entitled: *Alice's Adventures Underground*, then *Alice's Hour in Elfland* and *Adventures in Wonderland* before *Alice's Adventures in Wonderland* was settled upon.

When he took up first-aid, he went to watch a man having his leg amputated to reassure himself that, in an emergency, he wouldn't faint at the sight of blood.

The Dean of Christ Church's daughter, Alice Liddell, for whom the book was written, unsentimentally sold the original manuscript which had been given to her by Carroll. It raised £15,000 at Sotheby's in 1928, when Alice was seventy-six years old.

Edward Lear, *nonsense-verse writer*

. . . was subject to epileptic fits, which he believed to be caused by his inability to stop masturbating.

He gave drawing lessons to Queen Victoria.

He caught syphilis as a young man in London and this seems to have put him off women for life. He later became a homosexual.

Doctor Samuel Johnson, *dictionary-compiler*

. . . was, incredible though it may seem, into flagellation and bondage. The old boy had a set of padlocks and fetters in which he allowed himself to be confined while his good friend Mrs Hester Thrale, a brewer's widow, applied the rod. As with so many who delight in the kiss of the whip, he had been thrashed as a boy – in his case, by a sadistic head master at Lichfield Grammar School.

Mrs Thrale may have been an unwilling partner in the bondage sessions. She wrote him a letter ending with the

16

words: 'Do not quarrel with your Governess for not using the rod enough.' A letter from him to her contained the following: 'I want you to hold me in that slavery which you know so well how to render pleasant . . .' Whew! (He also liked to kneel down and kiss her foot.)

All this from an overweight, gout-ridden old chap who was blind in one eye and deaf in one ear. He had suffered from scrofula as a child and had been taken to London to receive the royal touch from Queen Anne in an attempt to cure it.

He also had a passion for cups of tea and once drank twenty-five cups, one after the other, in a house to which he had been invited.

He was nothing if not experimental. He shaved all the hairs off his arms and chest to see how long it would take for them to grow back again.

He was immensely strong. When he found a man sitting in his seat at the theatre, and the interloper refused to budge, he picked up man and chair and hurled them into the pit.

At the age of sixty, he climbed a tree which he had once climbed as a child, just to prove that he could still do it.

William Wordsworth, *Lakeland poet*

. . . ironically, for one who wrote so much about flowers, had no sense of smell.

He was so depressed about his career at one time in his life that he seriously considered becoming a tramp.

On a holiday to Paris just after the French Revolution, he stole a piece of the Bastille as a souvenir.

He left a souvenir of his own behind in the shape of an illegitimate baby daughter called Caroline – the result of an affair between himself and a French girl named Annette Vallon.

The act of writing poems caused him physical pain in his side.

He terrified many a rambler and unsuspecting passer-by on the moors and fells of the Lake District by his habit of composing his poems as he walked along, then booming them out loudly at the top of his voice.

Some authorities think that he may have had more than just a brotherly love for his sister Dorothy, with whom he lived for many years and who continued to be part of the household even when the poet married.

When Dorothy and he went on holiday in the West Country, the locals, on account of their strange northern accent and their habit of taking nocturnal rambles, thought they were French spies and alerted the Home Office as to their presence. This resulted in their being followed by a secret agent, who reported their every move and conversation.

He was once highly critical of the Lakes. He wrote: 'I begin to wish much to be in town. Cataracts and mountains are good occasional society, but they will not do for constant companions.'

He was in the habit of taking his false teeth out in the evening, causing his family and visitors to have great difficulty in understanding what he was saying.

Percy Bysshe Shelley, *poet*

. . . was addicted to sailing paper boats on ponds and large puddles. Whenever he came to a suitable stretch of water, he would fold up pieces of paper in the shape of a boat and float them lovingly round and round. If he couldn't find a piece of paper, he would take a large banknote out of his pocket and use that.

Whilst on holiday at Lynmouth, he devised eccentric methods of disseminating his radical broadsheet *Declar-*

ution of Rights. He popped copies into bottles and threw them into the sea. He also sent them out in little miniature boats and small hot-air balloons made out of silk globes with a little wick underneath.

He was extremely clumsy. He was always tripping up and falling over carpets, lawns and down stairs. Climbing up the stairs, he would frequently slip and bruise his nose and lips against the upper steps.

He delighted in terrorizing small children by telling them scary stories or pretending to be a monster.

During his schooldays at Eton, he tried to raise the Devil with the aid of a skull and he gave his housemaster an electric shock by wiring his doorknob up to a machine that generated electricity.

He once fled from a room in which Lord Byron was reciting poetry after seeing a vision of a woman with eyes instead of nipples.

He was a lifelong hypochondriac and sleepwalker. In 1813, he fancied he had caught elephantiasis (a disease in which parts of the body become extremely large and swollen). He compared his skin with other people to see how far the condition had advanced. At a country dance, he went so far as to walk along a line of young girls feeling their breasts to see (so he said) if they had contracted it too.

Algernon Charles Swinburne, *poet*

. . . enjoyed being whipped by prostitutes in St John's Wood, London. His taste for such pleasures was first aroused by the numerous bare-bottomed floggings he received at Eton.

His poetry is full of flagellatory themes. One of his longest poems is entitled 'The Flogging Block' by Rufus Rodworthy, with annotations by Barebum Birchingham.

Whilst living on the Isle of Wight, he had sexual

relations with a monkey, which he dressed as a woman. When it became jealous of a young man friend and tried to bite him, he had it grilled and served for lunch.

When he lived with the painter Rossetti at his house in Chelsea, he caused his host great embarrassment by sliding down the bannister stark naked into a room full of people and walking round the house on several occasions in a similar state of undress.

He once had an epileptic fit in the artist Whistler's studio and had to be revived by none other than Whistler's mother.

When agitated, he displayed some strange mannerisms, such as holding his arms stiffly by his side and waggling his fingers, or jerking his legs wildly in all directions.

Rossetti, worried that Algernon had never slept with a member of the opposite sex, bribed the five-times wed actress Adah Menken £10 to seduce the poet. After spending the night with Swinburne, she gave Rossetti the money back saying: 'I can't make him understand that *biting's* no use . . .'

Dante Gabriel Rossetti, *pre-Raphaelite painter*

. . . liked animals – not just the odd Towser or Tabby, but a whole menagerie, which he kept in his backyard at Chelsea. It consisted of squirrels, hedgehogs, peacocks, owls, a raccoon, wallabies, kangaroos, mice, marmots – and an armadillo, which burrowed underground to surface in the kitchen of the house next door. This caused a great affright among the servants, who screamed and ran out thinking that the Devil was rising out of the bowels of hell.

He once owned a wombat which regularly ate at the dinner table but suddenly went missing. It was later found dead in a cigar-box.

He was strongly attracted to girls with red or blonde hair and would pounce on them in the street and ask them to sit for him. He painted his red-haired wife Lizzie as the drowned Ophelia while she was lying in a water-filled tin bath.

When Lizzie died in 1862, probably by her own hand, as a romantic gesture he placed all his poems under her hair in the coffin. Seven years later, after being urged to have them published, he found he could not remember the words. Consequently, he had his wife's corpse exhumed from its grave in Highgate Cemetery, and the poems were retrieved and disinfected.

Leonardo da Vinci, *painter and all-round genius*

. . . was fascinated by ugly people and would follow them around all day.

He was a homosexual who, at the age of twenty-three, had been brought before the court in Florence accused of sodomy.

To further his knowledge of anatomy, he dissected patients who had died at his local hospital – sometimes only hours after talking to them on their deathbed.

James Abbott McNeill Whistler, *American artist*

. . . was a racial bigot – he hated blacks and Jews. On a ship bound for England from South America, he took exception to a black man on the grounds of his colour and for no reason kicked him across the deck of the ship and down some stairs. The captain confined him to his cabin for the rest of the voyage.

He was highly affected in his dress. He carried two umbrellas, one black, one white, and had pink bows on his shoes.

When invited out to dinner, he was prone to fall asleep at the table.

Fond of brawling, he once knocked his brother-in-law through a plate-glass window.

When he got into serious debt in London, he worked his charm on the bailiffs who called at his house in Tite Street to serve writs. Instead, they found themselves serving Sunday breakfast to him on promise of future payment for their services.

As old age advanced, he lied about his age and wore make-up. He also wore black velvet pantaloons and diamond buckles on his shoes, and was fond of white suits topped with a white stove-pipe hat. He sported a monocle, which he dropped from his eye to emphasize a witty remark.

As he grew even more impoverished, after bailiffs took his furniture, he would paint a picture of the missing item of furniture on the floor in its place.

The correct title of his most famous portrait, known universally as 'Whistler's Mother' is 'Arrangement in Grey and Black No 1: The Artist's Mother'.

Alfred Tennyson, *Poet Laureate*

. . . started composing lines of poetry at five years old.

As a child, he had the disquieting habit of lying flat out among the graves outside the church where his father was rector and wishing he were dead. He also fell into mysterious trances.

He had a fear of insanity and epilepsy, which ran in the family, and sometimes contemplated suicide because of it.

He was extremely short-sighted and would thrust his face into other people's faces in order to scrutinize them closely.

He had a talent for odd pieces of mimicry, and among his various party pieces were impersonations of a man sitting on the lavatory and a bird sitting in a tree.

When presented to Queen Victoria on being appointed Poet Laureate, he wore a borrowed suit – the very same one that William Wordsworth had borrowed from a mutual friend, Samuel Rogers, on becoming Poet Laureate in 1845. There was only one snag as regards the fit of the suit – Tennyson was eight inches taller than Rogers.

For one with a staid Victorian image, he had bouts of unconventional behaviour – such as the time he lay full-length on the floor and asked a lady to use him as a footstool.

He suffered from gout and wore surgical stockings to help his varicose veins.

His fame and reputation were taken advantage of in the most shameless manner by the makers of Cockles' Pills in a newspaper testimonial purporting to have been sent to

23

them by Tennyson himself, which read: *'Dear Sirs, Like most literary men, I am subject to violent constipation and your pills I find of the utmost comfort. A. Tennyson.'*

Sir Edwin Landseer, *Victorian artist*

. . . was ambidextrous – he could sketch with either hand at the same time.

On being commissioned to sculpture the Trafalgar Square lions in 1859, he used as a model a dead lion from Regent's Park Zoo which was delivered, still warm, to his home in St John's Wood. The corpse arrived during dinner with some friends and its arrival was announced by his po-faced manservant, who entered the dining room and solemnly enquired: 'Did you order a lion, sir . . .?'

When the lions were first displayed at the foot of Nelson's Column, a man, subsequently arrested as a lunatic, bombarded them with stones.

In later life, Landseer became an alcoholic and suffered from DTs.

Sadly, he also had periods of madness. On visiting the Duchess of Abercorn's aged mother, who was bedfast with bronchitis, he sat on the old lady's chest – almost suffocating her by his vast bulk – and was only persuaded to rise when she was on the point of blacking out completely.

Oscar Wilde, *writer and wit*

. . . when about to be mugged by three Parisian robbers, invited them to the nearest café, where they sat laughing at his wit for two hours and paid for all his drinks.

Thomas Hardy, *poet and novelist*

. . . had a love of cats. In his home, Max Gate, planks were placed to form a bridge between items of furniture so that the pampered pussies could travel round the room without having to touch the floor. Usually though, his cats met the same sad end – cut in two on a nearby railway line. He always gave the halves a solemn burial in the back garden, their pathetic little graves topped with engraved tombstones.

When he was a baby, he was found sound asleep in his cot with a snake curled up beside him.

His first wife Emma started to become mentally unstable towards the end of her life and began to fancy that Hardy was Dr Crippen (whom he resembled), adding that she expected to find herself dead in the cellar one morning. She reported him to the police, who took no action.

On Christmas Eve, 1919, as he was placing holly on his grandfather's grave in a churchyard, he saw a ghost dressed in the style of the eighteenth century which spoke to him, saying: 'A green Christmas . . .'

Rudyard Kipling, *author*

. . . had a hatred of telephones and would not have one in his house. All urgent business with him had to be done through telegrams.

Edgar Allan Poe, *American horror-story writer*

. . . won first prize for the best poem and story submitted to the *Baltimore Visitor*. He turned up at the award ceremony in a scruffy frock-coat buttoned to the throat to conceal his lack of a shirt and a pair of dilapidated boots into which were thrust his stockingless feet.

Voltaire, *French writer and wit*

. . . attempted many odd cures for his chronic constipation. A quack doctor advised him to swallow lead shot on the grounds that this was how glass bottles were washed out. He went through agonizing pain after following this rather dubious advice, but somehow survived.

In Germany, he became addicted to extra-strong laxative pills and begged the King of Prussia to send him a pound of them when he was home in France.

He was an enema freak – never going anywhere without the contraption with which he administered the enemas.

When he contracted smallpox, doctors gave him as a cure eight emetics and 100 quarts of lemonade.

As a reaction against all this unorthodox medical attention, he suffered from dizziness, poor hearing and eyesight, and all his teeth dropped out.

Modern-day health fanatics would also be horrified at his prodigious caffeine intake. He drank twenty cups of coffee in a single afternoon and as much as fifty cups a day. He also liked to mix tea with coffee and drank cup after cup of this unholy alliance. This gave him chronic indigestion and he slept little more than five hours a night.

He wrote a great deal in bed – sometimes spending up to sixteen hours a day there.

He had an incestuous relationship with his niece, the actress Marie-Louise Denis.

When bored by uninteresting visitors, he would pretend to faint in order to get rid of them.

His odd tastes continued to the end. A newspaper reported that on his deathbed, he became so delirious that he 'put his hand in his chamber-pot, drew out what was in it and *ate* it . . .'

Victor Hugo, *French novelist and poet*

. . . wrote all his books in a standing position. He claimed that when an author wrote sitting down 'the blood sinks to his arse when it should remain in his head. Too many write with their arses.'

He also wrote in the nude. When he needed to concentrate fully in order to finish a book, he ordered his servant to hide all his clothes so that he would be unable to wander abroad – thus making sure all his efforts were directed towards his work.

He wrote at a furious pace – wearing out several quills a week.

He had an enormous appetite and he finished off his many-course meals by eating up to six oranges – *complete with peel*.

An epic womanizer, even in his seventies he had scores of affairs including one with the young actress Sarah Bernhardt, fifty years his junior. He was still engaged in sex up to his death at eighty-three.

His brother Eugene went mad at Victor's marriage to Adèle, whom Eugene secretly loved. He was taken straight from the wedding reception to a lunatic asylum, where he remained until he died.

Exiled from France, Victor became a major tourist attraction at his home in Guernsey, not so much because of his literary reputation but chiefly for his habit of every day at noon taking all his clothes off on the verandah and pouring buckets of cold water over his head – after which he would rub himself vigorously all over his naked body with a pair of rough gloves.

He held table-rapping seances in which he claimed to have discussed theology with Jesus himself.

Ludwig van Beethoven, *composer*

. . . was naturally very clumsy. He was always breaking crockery and ornaments and walking into furniture. His face after shaving was a mass of cuts.

He dressed so shabbily that he was once arrested as a tramp and, despite his protestations, no one would believe that he was the great Beethoven.

At a restaurant, when a waiter brought him the wrong meal, he picked up the dish in a temper and chucked it in the waiter's face.

When he started to go deaf, he resorted to the use of an ear-trumpet.

Richard Kirwan, *Irish scholar and president of the Irish Academy*

. . . had an obsessive fear of flies and would pay his servants a reward for the corpse of each fly they killed and brought to him.

He always wore a hat, whether indoors or out, and walked round with a pet eagle perched on his shoulder.

Sir Thomas More, *author of Utopia*

. . . beheaded by Henry VIII for refusing to take the Oath of Supremacy, he advocated that couples should see each other stark naked before marrying. When Sir William

Roper came to him with a proposal to marry one of his daughters, he took him to the chambers where two of them lay asleep and whipped back the bedsheets, revealing the two young girls with their smocks up to their armpits. Awaking with a start, they turned their backs for decency's sake, to which Sir Bill replied: 'I have seen both sides now' – then patted the girl he chose to marry on the bare bum.

George Sand, *French writer*

. . . was a woman who started to dress like a man while in Paris because, she claimed, her mother told her it was cheaper than buying Parisian women's clothes. The real reason was because she was a dominant lesbian who smoked cigars.

Maurice Baring, *English novelist*

. . . when invited to dinner, had the habit of sitting through the meal with a glass of port balanced on top of his bald head.

When told by his aunt that his pince-nez didn't suit him, he removed them from his nose and tossed them on the fire.

He would startle people by rushing from a crowded room and jumping fully clothed into the nearest pool or pond.

Once, as a prank, he persuaded a friend's wife to have herself wrapped in brown paper and placed on the luggage-rack of a train. The ticket-inspector fled, horrified, after hearing giggles emanating from the large 'parcel' on the rack.

Sir Thomas Malory, *writer*

. . . the author of the medieval romance *Morte d'Arthur*, with its tales of great chivalry at the court of King Arthur, was quite the opposite himself. He was a rapist, horse-thief, cattle-rustler, housebreaker, leader of a band of robbers and an extortionist.

He wrote most of the book – a bestseller of the time – whilst in prison, where he spent a great deal of his life.

Samuel Pepys, *diarist*

. . . liked his little bit on the side. His wife once walked into a room and caught him feeling up the maid, who was then sacked. Sam found out where the girl had moved to, then took her out in a carriage and took up from where he had left off.

While sat in the window of a London wine-house with his lover – linen-seller Betty Lane – he started to grope her with such abandon that a passer-by threw a stone at the window and told him to desist immediately. Sam scuttled off red-faced through a back exit.

He loved to buy pornographic material, which he would read while masturbating – recording his masturbations in his famous diary with special symbols.

His wife blackmailed him to the tune of £400 – threatening to tell the world at large about his affairs if he didn't pay up.

A vain man, he kept his face smooth by rubbing it with a pumice-stone.

Zane Grey, *author*

. . . his Christian name wasn't really Zane. It was *Pearl*. Not surprisingly, this prolific author of macho westerns found himself another more masculine name with which to adorn the title page.

Jonathan Swift, *satirist*

. . . could read the entire Bible when only five years old.

He never laughed in company and claimed he had only laughed twice in his whole life.

An early jogging fanatic, he ran up and down the hills near his home. When the weather was bad, he ran up and down the stairs for hour after hour.

G. K. Chesterton, *novelist and essayist*

. . . was notoriously absent-minded. He once set off for an important dinner dressed in evening clothes and a pair of cycling shoes. In a café, while making rather grand gestures to a friend with long sweeps of his arm, he inadvertently swept his two poached eggs off the plate and into his lap. Summoning the waitress, he ordered two more, saying sadly: 'I seem to have lost the first two . . .'

When writing at his home, if he suffered a mental block he would fire arrows from a bow through the window at trees outside.

He was a large, buoyant individual who wore a sombrero-like hat and a cloak. He never went out without a veritable armoury – a dagger, swordstick and pistol.

He wrote on the hoof, as it were – in pubs, cabs, on the tops of buses, in restaurants and against the walls of buildings in busy streets.

He was loved by cab drivers for his habit of hiring a cab to go a journey of a few yards . . . then keeping the driver on hire for several hours before emerging from a pub or restaurant to make the equally short return journey.

Oliver Goldsmith, *Irish writer*

. . . was once found by a fellow student at college lying up to his chin in feathers in his bedroom. Red-faced, he explained that on the preceding evening, he had met a woman with five children who had told him a sob story about her husband being in hospital and that she was a poor country girl with no food or shelter for her offspring. Whether or not that was true, Goldsmith was touched by the tale and brought her back to the college, where he gave her some of his clothes to sell and even the blankets off his bed to cover the children. During the night, finding himself very cold, he had cut open his bed and buried himself among the feathers to keep warm.

He was a vain man. After a visit to a puppet show in London, when a friend commented how well one of the little puppets had jumped over a stick, he exclaimed: 'Pshaw! I can do it better myself.' On demonstrating the superiority of human beings over puppets, he slipped and broke his leg.

W. S. Gilbert, *librettist*

. . . was abducted at the age of two by kidnappers in Naples and returned to his parents only when they paid a ransom of £25.

He was frightened of high speeds – his chauffeur was never allowed to drive the car at more than 20 miles an hour.

He drowned at the age of seventy-four in a lake he had made at the back of his house. He had been attempting to rescue a girl who had got into difficulties in the water.

Daniel Defoe, *author of Robinson Crusoe*

. . . was a government spy. In the reign of Queen Anne, he travelled all over the country building up his spy network, thus laying the foundations of the British Secret Service.

His real name wasn't Defoe – it was simply Daniel *Foe*. He added the 'De' because he thought it sounded more sophisticated.

He was once placed in the pillory for 'a horrible slander on the Church'. His 'wanted' poster describes him as being 'a middle-sized, spare man of a brown complexion, dark brown coloured hair but wears a wig; a hooked nose, a sharp chin, grey eyes and a large mole near his mouth'.

L. S. Lowry, *artist*

. . . wore shabby, threadworn clothes even when he became wealthier towards the end of his life. They were often covered with food and drink stains. When asked what he did with his old suits, he replied: 'I *wear* them . . .'

Sir Walter Scott, *Scottish novelist*

. . . was plagued by unsolicited manuscripts from would-be authors. On one occasion, he received an extremely large parcel from the United States for which he had to pay

£5 postage. It contained a play from a young lady in New York, entitled *The Cherokee Lovers* and a letter begging him to read and correct it, write a prologue and epilogue, have it put on the stage at Drury Lane and negotiate for the copyright. Two weeks later, he received another parcel for which he had to pay a further £5 from the same lady. It was another copy of *The Cherokee Lovers* sent by the same lady, who feared that as the weather had been stormy, the first manuscript might have been lost in the post.

James Harrington, *seventeenth-century political theorist*

. . . was the author of *Oceana*, in which he outlined his ideas for a commonwealth. He also imagined that his sweat could turn into flies – and sometimes bees. To test his bizarre theory, he had a timber house built in a garden belonging to a friend who lived facing St James's Park in London. In the full heat of the sun, he would sit inside it (after first taking the precaution of swatting all the flies already in residence). After half an hour or so, when the flies which had escaped the massacre by lurking in nooks and crannies in the woodwork started to emerge from their hiding-places and buzz around his head, he would exclaim triumphantly: 'Do you not see it apparent that *these* come from me?'

Francis Bacon, *Elizabethan statesman, philosopher and author*

. . . had a strange affinity for rain. During springtime showers, he rode round London in an open coach, letting the rain soak him thoroughly. He claimed that the rain was wholesome because of 'the Nitre in the air and the Universal spirit of the world.'

Aesop, *Greek fable writer*

. . . was a small writer of tall tales – he measured under three and a half feet in height.

Auguste Rodin, *French sculptor*

. . . one night left open the window of his studio, in which he was modelling in clay a large statue of the French writer Victor Hugo amid The Muses. A storm blew in and made the bottom part of the clay a soggy mass. When Rodin entered the room next morning with a number of arty friends, they acclaimed the work as a 'masterpiece of masterpieces' – in particular his theme of Hugo rising from a bed of slime to conquer all.

Giacomo Casanova, *Italian author of lewd nature*

. . . had an odd taste in practical jokes. Once, as a revenge for a ducking he received in a prank, he dug up a fresh corpse and cut an arm off it. He then hid under his fellow-prankster's bed and tugged at the sheets. The victim, suspecting Casanova was up to his tricks, sneered that he wasn't afraid of ghosts and he reached under the bed to grab hold of Casanova, who handed him the severed arm. The poor man, on seeing the gruesome limb, had a stroke and became paralysed for life as a result.

His favourite recommended method of contraception was to cut a lemon in half, scoop out all the flesh and insert it into the woman's vagina like a Dutch cap.

He used to grow the nail on his little finger extra long so that he could pick the wax out of his ears with it.

He delighted in making love while being watched by other people or having sex with two women at a time. (One after the other, of course.)

Samuel Boyce, *eighteenth-century Irish poet*

. . . was subject to a strange mixture of indolence and prodigality. His speciality was writing begging letters, the income from which barely kept his wife and child. When the begging letters failed to bring any monetary response, he would send out his wife to tell his friends that he was dying, in the hope that they would give her some money in pity.

He became so poor that he eventually pawned nearly all his clothes and took to his bed with the one blanket he had left.

When he ventured out, he did so in a shirt he had fashioned out of paper, a long, tatty coat and no trousers.

When his long-suffering wife died, he could not afford mourning apparel, so he bought a piece of black ribbon and tied it round the family's pet dog.

Havelock Ellis, *sexologist*

. . . married a lesbian. He was also impotent for much of his life.

He liked to watch women urinating and persuaded his lover Françoise Lafitte to pee whilst walking in the rain down the street and also in the middle of a packed Oxford Circus.

He asked his women friends for photographs of them taken in the nude, and women all over the world sent him pictures of themselves in the buff.

For twelve years he kept a note of all his dirty dreams and, like Samuel Pepys, kept a secret note in his diary of his masturbations.

He took the hallucinogenic drug mescaline in the form of mescal buttons and saw visions of jewels and butterflies.

Marquis de Sade, *sadist*

. . . wrote porno novels in the Bastille after being imprisoned there.

During a visit to a brothel in Marseilles, he gave the prostitutes chocolates laced with Spanish fly, which caused two of them to die and a third to jump out of a window.

He whipped a girl named Rose Keller with knotted cords after tying her naked to a bed, then poured hot sealing wax into the wounds.

Not surprisingly, he died in a lunatic asylum at the age of seventy-four.

2
Monstrous Regiment

Wherein we meet Marie Stopes and her consideration for endangered genitalia . . . the actress who poked corpses . . . the odd occupation of Frances Farmer . . . Cleopatra's bizarre cure for baldness . . . what Mae West did with a xylophone player for nine hours non-stop . . . and the prostitute who ate her night's wages for breakfast.

'Women are ever in extremes; they are either better or worse than men.' *Jean de la Bruyère (1645–1696)*

Marie Stopes, *British birth control pioneer*

. . . believed that all men should wear kilts because of the damage that the rubbing of trousers could cause to the genitals. With this in mind, she made her young son walk around in a knitted skirt.

For a birth control pioneer she displayed incredible naïvety. She did not know what masturbation was until she was twenty-nine.

She believed in the efficacy of sea water as an aid to good health and drank several glasses of it every day.

During a miners' strike in the 1920s, she wrote to the prime minister, Lloyd George, offering to storm the miners' headquarters with a band of armed men. Holding guns to the heads of the miners' leaders, she would force them to send out notices to their men to go back to work. The PM politely declined her proposal.

An early aficionado of Women's Lib, she wrote to Rudyard Kipling to try and persuade him to amend the last line of his famous poem 'If' from '. . . you'll be a Man, my son!' to something else – on the grounds that it left out all mention of women and was therefore unfair to them.

She started the first-ever (and probably the last) birth control clinic in a horse-drawn caravan, which was intended to travel the country dispensing contraceptive advice to the ladies of Britain. The scheme came to a premature conclusion when the caravan was burned down by a toffee-shop assistant in Bradford.

When her home in the country was bombed twice in the Second World War, she was convinced that it had been on the personal orders of Goering himself.

Sarah Bernhardt, *French actress*

. . . never used a wooden leg, despite having her leg amputated. When taking part in plays, she would prop herself against the furniture onstage. She preferred to be carried about in a specially made chair, rather than have a false limb.

She had an obsession with death. She made visits to dissecting rooms to look at corpses, which she prodded with her parasol.

She took her coffin on tour with her, sometimes sleeping in it at night. It had been a present from her mother and she was eventually laid to rest in it.

Clara Bow, *the 'It' girl*

. . . if the 'It' in question was stamina, she certainly had her share as she is said to have listed among her sexual conquests *the entire football team of the University of California in Los Angeles*.

She had her two pet dogs dyed red to match her hair.

Nell Gwynn, *mistress of Charles II*

. . . was brought up in a brothel and later worked as a barmaid in a similar establishment.

Josephine Baker, *entertainer*

. . . took a panther to dine with her at Maxim's restaurant in Paris. When the waiter brought the caviar she had ordered for it, the panther bit his arm.

She also took a cheetah to see *Aida* at the Paris Opéra. It jumped into the pit and mauled the conductor.

Florence Nightingale, *nurse*

. . . heard a voice. Not just anyone's voice, you understand, but the voice of God himself. She claimed he had spoken to her four times in her life, calling her to his service.

She had the disconcerting habit of going into a trance-like state – sometimes while in the middle of dinner and often for hours on end.

While touring the hospital wards, she carried in her

pocket a pet owl named Athena, which was subject to fits.

In later life, she became a hypochondriac and spent long periods in bed.

In 1857, she became so convinced that she was going to die that she made all the arrangements for her own funeral. They weren't needed until she actually *did* die – *fifty-three years later!*

Cleopatra, *Queen of Egypt*

. . . had a hooked nose and a large mouth.

Was the author of a book on cosmetics, which included a recipe for hair loss. Among the ingredients were burnt mice, bear-grease and honey, to be rubbed on to the bald spot 'until it sprouts . . .'

Her boyfriend Mark Antony was a womanizer and a drunkard. Once, after an all-night carousal following a wedding ceremony, he went into the Roman forum and threw up into his toga. It's a wonder what they saw in one another . . .

Frances Farmer, *film star*

. . . was arrested by the police for running topless through a hotel. On the charge-sheet, she gave her occupation as 'cock-sucker'.

She was put into an asylum after hearing voices and claimed to have been beaten and raped while inside.

Kitty Fisher, *eighteenth-century top society prostitute*

. . . charged 100 guineas a night for her company. When Edward, Duke of York, paid her only 50 guineas, she showed her disgust by taking the £50 banknote, putting it between two slices of bread and eating it for breakfast.

She was painted by Sir Joshua Reynolds.

Joan Crawford, *film star*

. . . had a mania for cleanliness and could often be seen on her hands and knees scrubbing the floor of her luxury home.

On entering, guests had to change into white slippers so as not to sully the luxurious and expensive white carpet.

When invited to dine with friends or out to a restaurant, she would take her own vodka – which was 100 per cent proof. She drank two pints of it a day.

She dressed two of her adopted children identically and called them 'the twins' – even though they came from different homes.

Mae West, *screen vamp*

. . . never actually said: 'Come up and see me sometime.' In the film *She Done Him Wrong*, what she said to Cary Grant was: 'Any time you got nuthin' to do – and lotsa time to do it – come on up . . .'

She was a diminutive 4 feet 11 inches in height.

Many people thought she was a man dressed as a woman.

She was sent to jail for corrupting the morals of youth when she appeared in a play she had written called *Sex*.

The RAF named an inflatable life-saving jacket after her in honour of her ample bosom.

She once claimed to have made love with a xylophone player for nine hours without stopping.

Anne Boleyn, *wife of Henry VIII*

. . . was flat-chested, had a tooth that stuck out from the rest, sported a large mole on her neck and had six fingers on one hand.

Anne of Bohemia, *wife of Richard II*

. . . introduced the crackpot custom of wearing shoes with toes so long that the ends had to be tied to the knees to prevent herself tripping over them.

Princess Margaret, *Queen Elizabeth II's sister*

. . . astonished the Governor of Kenya in 1956 by responding to his courteous leave-taking bow with a cheery: 'See ya later, alligator.' The Governor, Sir Evelyn Baring, confused by the remark, had to have it explained to him by an aide that the correct response should have been: 'In a while, crocodile . . .'

Lady (Emma) Hamilton, *Nelson's mistress*

. . . had an early career as a prostitute in London. She later worked for a quack doctor, James Gordon, as his

Goddess of Health. This involved performing nude dances around a 'Celestial Bed', which was rented out to childless couples for £50 a night as a supposed cure for infertility.

She had a daughter, Horatia, by Nelson, although at the time she was married to Sir William Hamilton, thirty-five years her senior, who knew nothing of the birth as she had cunningly hidden her pregnant state under voluminous skirts.

After the naval hero's death at Trafalgar, she became an alcoholic, went to jail for debt and died a bloated wreck at the age of fifty near Calais.

Pauline Bonaparte, *Napoleon's sister*

... was an insatiable adultress. Her Italian husband Camillo Borghese had a tiny problem – his penis. It was so small that he could not keep her faithful to him.

It is thought that among her many lovers was her famous brother himself.

An affair she had with a painter named De Forbin nearly finished her off. His problem was the exact opposite of her husband's – his penis was so enormous that it caused internal damage and left her thoroughly exhausted.

She bathed daily in five gallons of milk, into which she was lowered naked by her husky Negro servant.

She was so vain that she died with a mirror in her hand.

3
Roman Rulers

Wherein we meet Julius Caesar and his bashfulness about baldness . . . Tiberius and his personal live sex shows . . . the cruel Caligula . . . Claudius and his edict on passing wind . . . and the Emperor who *would* hurt a fly.

'Rome wasn't built in a day.' *Barratus Homeses*

Julius Caesar

. . . although a prodigious womanizer, also had homosexual proclivities (he swung both ways, as the saying goes today). When he was a young man in the army, he had a gay relationship with King Nicomedes of Bithynia for which he was taunted in later life.

A bit of a fop, he was very sensitive about his balding head and used to try to cover it up by combing the little hair he had left over it (*à la* Bobby Charlton and Arthur Scargill). He was highly delighted when the Senate voted him the privilege of wearing a laurel wreath and took to wearing it at every opportunity to hide his thinning locks.

He was an epileptic and he also suffered from nightmares.

On being confronted by his assassins with their daggers drawn, his main concern was that he should die with

propriety. He undid the belt on the bottom part of his gown so that it would fall and cover up his legs as he lay dead on the ground.

Augustus

. . . even as an old man he enjoyed nothing better than deflowering virgins . . . which were sometimes provided for him by his thoughtful wife.

An insomniac, he employed a man to tell him bedtime stories to make him fall asleep.

He hated having his hair cut and would have as many as three barbers cutting his hair simultaneously.

Once a year, he would go out on to the streets of Rome pretending to be a beggar.

He had an odd superstition, inasmuch as he would only begin long journeys on drizzly days.

Tiberius

. . . was a real sexual all-rounder and a voyeur-extraordinary. On the Isle of Capri, he had teams of specially trained beautiful young men and women, called *spintrae*, who would perform sexual gymnastics and copulate in a variety of positions in front of him to arouse his passion. Similarly, he loved them to dress up as Pans and nymphs to fornicate for him in woodland glades.

When he went swimming in the nude, he would take along small boys, whom he called his 'minnows' and trained to swim alongside him darting in and out like little fish, nibbling and licking him between the legs. He also enjoyed having fellatio performed on him by unweaned babies.

Once, at a sacrificial ceremony, he took a shine to the sacred trumpeter and his brother the incense-swinger. In a cloud of lust, he rushed them out of the temple and had his way with them. When they registered a protest at this unseemly treatment, he had their legs broken.

He also had a penchant for cunnilingus, which he practised on the high-ranking ladies of the court, whether they wanted to or not. One lady stabbed herself to death rather than face the tongue treatment from Tiberius.

He was also cruel, with a sadistic streak of humour. When startled by a fisherman at his retreat in Capri, the man said he had merely wished to present his emperor with a large mullet. Incensed by this intrusion into his privacy, Tiberius ordered his guards to rub the fish into the man's face, which they did – skinning his face raw in the process. When the fisherman cried: 'Thank heaven I didn't bring the emperor the large crab I caught!' Tiberius sent for the crab – and had that rubbed into his face too!

Caligula

. . . led a life which was a catalogue of cruelty. As part of the attraction at his vicious games, he would order physically handicapped people to fight one another or match old-age pensioners against equally ancient animals. To economize on his butcher's bill, he kept his wild animals fed with criminals.

He ordered mothers and fathers to be present at the executions of their sons and daughters, and after one such occasion, attempted to make one grieving father laugh by telling him jokes.

His meals were enlivened by the sight of people being tortured while he ate.

He was crazy about money and liked to walk barefoot over mounds of gold coins, then lounge languidly upon them.

Incitatus, his favourite horse, received better treatment than his wife Caesonia, whom he liked to display naked in front of his friends. The horse slept in a marble stable with ivory stalls and purple blankets. It was provided with a team of servants and a house in which to entertain 'guests'.

He had a taste for buggery with a wide range of men, from young nobles to foreign prisoners.

He liked to invite couples of high station to dine with him, then rush the wife off to his bedroom and ravish her – commenting afterwards to the assembled diners how she had performed sexually in bed.

He indulged himself incestuously with his three sisters and regarded one of them, Drusilla, as a wife.

Tall, thin and hollow-eyed, he was terrified of thunder – hiding under his bed whenever a storm approached.

Claudius

. . . seems to have been a human Aunt Sally, on the receiving end of a variety of missiles. He was the butt of many a joke, and was bombarded with olive and date stones whenever he fell asleep at dinner.

Once, during a grain shortage, he was pelted with stale bread by a mob in the forum.

In court, when Claudius admitted the evidence of a prostitute against a Roman noble, the man chucked a set of wax tablets into his face, along with a stylus, badly gashing his cheek.

He had the habits of slobbering, stammering, laughing uncontrollably, running at the nose and twitching his head violently.

He passed a law sanctioning the breaking of wind 'either silently or noisily' at the dining table, after hearing of a man who had caused himself to be ill through restraining from farting at dinner.

Nero

. . . was a blue-eyed blond who thought that there was truly no business like showbusiness. In Naples, on his first public appearance as a singer, when an earthquake shook the theatre, he ignored it and sang his piece through without stopping.

To strengthen his naturally feeble voice, he took enemas to keep his weight down and lay with lead weights on his chest!

He took his own personal claque with him – five thousand in all – to applaud his performances and the gates were locked to prevent anyone leaving.

His sexual excesses knew no bounds – he coupled with

boys, other men's wives, the Vestal Virgins and his mother.

After castrating his favourite boy, Sporus, he married him and took him as his empress, dressing him in female attire.

In his lavish palace, he had a statue of himself in the entrance hall – 120 feet tall.

Vespasian

. . . had a curious facial expression which made him look as though he were constantly straining on the lavatory. When he asked a certain joker why he had never made up a joke about himself (Vespasian, that is), the man quipped: 'I will – when you have finished relieving yourself . . .'

Domitian

. . . like many a man made good, he tried to hide his humble origins. Notwithstanding his claim that he had been born in the Temple of the Flavians, his actual birthplace was a house in Pomegranate Street.

On becoming emperor, he spent hours on end catching flies and impaling them on his needle-sharp pen. Once, when a member of his household was asked if there was anyone with the emperor, he cracked: 'Nobody – not even a fly . . .'

At the gladiatorial games, his constant companion was a young lad with a curiously small head who was dressed all in red. He would hold long, serious debates with the boy, often discussing important matters of state with him and seeking his advice.

Like other Roman rulers, he was sensitive about his bald head, and any reference whatsoever to bald men, however innocent, he regarded as a personal insult. Those going thin on top might like to consult his manual entitled *Care of the Hair*.

4

Kings and Queens of England and Britain

Wherein we explore the cock-ups of William the Conqueror . . . the red-hot end of Edward II . . . the flashing of Queen Elizabeth I . . . the king who ended up as a salt-cellar . . . the monarch who expired on the royal lavatory . . . the king who danced with an admiral . . . Queen Victoria having hysterics . . . and the king who used the same collar-stud for fifty years.

'A crown, golden in show, is but a wreath of thorns; brings danger, troubles, cares and sleepless nights to him who wears a regal diadem.' *John Milton (1608–1674)*

William the Conqueror

. . . caused consternation among his Norman followers by his cock-ups before the Battle of Hastings. As he stepped ashore, he slipped and fell full-length with his arms outstretched. He tried to pass it off as a joke by grabbing the sand in both hands and claiming he would grab hold of England the same way. While preparing to arm himself for the fray, he inadvertently put his coat of mail on back to

56

front. This, he assured his superstitious soldiery, signified great change – his change of title from duke to king. Nice one, Bill . . .

There were even more slapstick scenes at his coronation on Christmas day 1066 in Westminster Abbey. At the moment of his crowning, a great cheer arose – but his troops guarding the abbey thought that a riot had started, endangering the life of the king and they set fire to nearby houses as a reprisal.

Having subdued the English with his Normans, the Normans who were left across the Channel wanted to free themselves from his yoke. By a strange irony, he then took an army of Englishmen to subdue the Normans.

He even fought his own son Robert in battle, though neither recognized the other underneath the armour they were dressed in. Robert clobbered his father and knocked him off his horse, and only realized whom he had struck when he heard William frantically shouting for help.

He and his wife Matilda must have looked an odd twosome when walking out together as he was 5 feet 10 inches while she was 4 feet 2 inches.

He died as a result of his own brutality. While sacking the French city of Mantes, he ordered all the houses to be fired. In a fateful act of poetic justice, his horse stood on a red-hot cinder, throwing the fat king against the pommel of his saddle and causing a fatal rupture.

Another version of how the Conqueror met his end is more colourful. It is known that he was a bit of a show-off and thought it a hoot to vault on to his horse while dressed in full armour to prove what a regular macho man he was. On the fateful occasion, claims one chronicler, he was so jubilant following the victory at Mantes, he performed the same cowboy-like feat – but his fatness threw him painfully against the pommel and resulted in the rupture.

The ludicrous aspect of his life followed him even unto death when, as his corpulent corpse was being forced into a sarcophagus palpably a few sizes too small, he burst and

caused such a stench that the clergy gabbled the service to a hasty conclusion as the mourners ran out holding their noses.

Edward II

. . . was a homosexual who came to an ironic and brutal end. As he was pressed face-down under a table at Berkeley Castle, his assassins pushed a horn up his anus, then shoved a red-hot poker up it, causing an agonizing disembowelment which left no outward signs of murder.

Henry II

. . . was a bull-necked redhead with an uncontrollably fiery temper. When angered, he would fling himself prostrate to the ground and chew frenziedly on the rushes that were used for floor-coverings. On one occasion, he leapt explosively out of his bed and proceeded to bung the stuffing out of his mattress into his mouth.

To do penance for the murder of Becket, he walked barefoot through Canterbury, prostrated himself before the saint's shrine, fasted for a day and a night, and then allowed the monks to whip him on his bare shoulders.

Richard II

. . . was a widower of twenty-nine when in 1396 he married Isabella, the daughter of the King of France. She was *eight years old* at the time.

Henry VI

. . . succeeded to the throne of England and France when he was only nine months old.

Queen Elizabeth I

. . . lost all her teeth because of her passion for cakes made with sticky currants and could only eat soup, gruel and soft food.

This led to a great deal of frustration among her courtiers, who couldn't understand her commands due to the fact that she spoke exceedingly quickly and with her lips wrapped round her gums.

In earlier life, when she possessed a set of gnashers, she made full use of them. In the 1570s, she and her court annually consumed 1,240 oxen; 8,200 sheep; 13,260 lambs; 2,752 dozen assorted poultry; 600,000 gallons of ale; 300 tuns of wine; 60,000 pounds of butter and 4,200,000 eggs.

Some historians have speculated that she might have been a hermaphrodite or suffered from some sexual deformity as a result of her father (Henry VIII) contracting syphilis.

For the first lady of the land, she had some ungentlemanly habits – which included spitting, beer-swilling and swearing. Her oaths were considered so violent that a Puritan named Fuller asked her permission to send her a book he had written, reproving her disgusting behaviour in that direction.

Her security system seems to have been very lax. When she was sixty-seven years old, she was accosted in her chamber by a knife-wielding drunken sailor who had written her a madly passionate love letter. When Dr William Parry was about to assassinate her in the Privy Garden, he only desisted at the last moment because she reminded him of her grandfather, Henry VII.

She seems also to have been something of a flasher. The French ambassador reported that during a private audience with her one day, she insisted for some reason on pulling open the front of her white damask dress a number of times so that he could see her stomach and belly button.

James I (VI of Scotland)

. . . was certainly no oil-painting if contemporary descriptions of him are anything approximating accuracy. Said one scribe: 'His beard was very thin. His tongue too large for his mouth, which made him speak full in the mouth and made him drink very uncomely as if eating his drink, which came out into the cup at each side of his mouth. His skin was soft as taffeta sarsnet, which felt so because he never washed his hands, only rubbed his fingers and slightly with the wet end of a napkin.'

In addition to all these endearing traits, he suffered from BO (or, to be more accurate, those standing next to him did) and his eyes would roll like marbles, causing great alarm to those at whom he was attempting to direct his gaze. His weak spindly legs caused him to lean heavily on whoever he was talking to, for support.

He was also a homosexual, lavishing his favourite, George Villiers, with honours. He addressed him as 'my sweet child and wife' and described himself as 'your old dad and husband'.

The son of Mary Queen of Scots, it was thought that her Italian secretary David Rizzio could have been his father. Consequently, as a boy, he was taunted by cries from rude people in the streets of 'Jimmy Davidson!' (i.e. Jimmy, son of David . . .).

He liked telling and listening to dirty jokes.

He once put a frog down the Earl of Pembroke's neck for a laugh.

As a hunter, he had the blood-lust, and on felling a deer, he would rip it open and put his arms and legs inside.

His perpetual fear of assassination led him to wear ridiculous-looking padded clothes full of thick quilted material which made him sweat profusely. Then he would have to take them off again and in doing so caught a lot of colds.

His bed was moved from room to room to confuse would-be regicides. Once, as he took an afternoon nap, some hunters let off their guns in a nearby field and he leapt frantically from his bed crying: 'Treason! Treason!' under the misapprehension that an attempt was being made on his life.

Charles I

. . . was small with very short legs caused by rickets as a child. This was due to a poor diet of curds and whey and a lack of sunlight.

He also spoke with a terrible stammer, which he attempted to correct by talking with pebbles in his mouth.

As a prince, he went on a jaunt to Spain with the Duke of Buckingham. They both wore false beards and called themselves Tom and John Smith.

There was a ghastly omen at his trial. He was leaning for support on his golden-headed staff when the head snapped and fell to the floor. He was later, of course, beheaded.

After his head was chopped off at Whitehall, gruesome souvenir hunters rushed to snatch hairs from the beard and dipped their handkerchiefs in his blood.

He wore two shirts to his execution as it was a cold day and he did not want anyone to think that he was shivering through fear.

A surgeon who did a post-mortem on his body 160 years after he died stole one of his vertebrae. The surgeon, Sir Henry Halford, then proudly used it at dinner parties as a salt-cellar. When Queen Victoria heard about it, she ordered him to return it to the king's coffin.

Charles II

. . . was always accompanied to the lavatory by two attendants – one to hold the candle and the other to hold the lavatory paper . . .

James II

. . . was thought to have been suffering from a sexually transmitted disease when he came to the throne, which was responsible for his extremely erratic behaviour.

Queen Mary II

. . . at the age of twelve, wrote strange passionate love letters to Frances Apsley – a woman of twenty – in which she took the part of a 'wife' to Frances's 'husband'. She wrote such hot stuff as: 'If all my hairs were lives, I would lose them all twenty times over to serve or satisfy you. Thou art my life, my soul, my all that Heaven can give . . .' (One has the feeling that, born 280 years later, she would have made a very capable Mills and Boon novelist.)

At the age of fifteen she married her cousin, William of Orange, who, let it be said, had a curiously close relationship with his former page, Hans William Bentinck, whom he later created Earl of Portland for services rendered. William believed that Bentinck had saved his life by sleeping in his bed when he contracted smallpox, thus drawing it out of William and into himself. He also had a mistress, Elizabeth Villiers – or 'Squinting Betty' as she was better known because of her eye defect.

When Mary became pregnant by William, she wrote to 'husband' Frances: 'I have played the whore a little. Because the sea parts us [she was in the Netherlands at the time] you may believe that it is a bastard.'

Queen Anne

. . . the podgy, gout-ridden sister of Queen Mary, also was enamoured of an older girl . . . namely Sarah Jennings, who was the wife-to-be of the great military campaigner John Churchill, the Duke of Marlborough.

In her heatedly affectionate letters, she adopted the pseudonym of 'Mrs Morley' while Sarah was 'Mrs Freeman'. When Anne came to the throne, Sarah was the power behind it with her strange hold over the queen – often upbraiding her in public.

She grew so fat that she had to be raised and lowered through trapdoors at Windsor Castle by means of ropes and pulleys.

George I

. . . was involved in an incredible murder and intrigue before he became king. He was married to Sophia Dorothea of Zell, who took a lover, Count Philip Christopher von Konigsmark. When George and his father, Ernest Augustus, the Elector of Hanover, found out, they had Konigsmark murdered. The unfortunate Sophia Dorothea was divorced, and imprisoned in the Castle of Ahlden for the next thirty-two years. As she paced the apartment in which she was destined to spend the rest of her life, little did she know that her dead former lover was still closer to her than she could ever have imagined. His corpse had been stuffed under the floorboards of her apartment.

George believed in keeping everything in the family. He had as his mistress his own half-sister the Baroness Kielmansegge, who was the daughter of Clara von Meisenbuch, his father's mistress. To complicate the love-tangle even more, he slept with Clara's sister Maria – that is, when his father wasn't sleeping with her. He was also the lover of the Countess von Platen, the wife of his half-brother.

To complete the picture, the murdered Count von Konigsmark (his ex-wife's ex-lover, remember?) had also been the lover of – you've guessed it – his father's mistress Clara von Meisenbuch.

When he died, yet another mistress – the Duchess of Kendal – believed that he had been reincarnated as a large black raven which had flown through the window of her home. He had told her that if there was a life after death, he would return and give her a sign. Obediently, she tended to the bird's every whim and accorded it the same respect as if it had been the king himself.

It is interesting to note that it was in George I's reign that a British prime minister had to discuss all business of state with his sovereign in *Latin*. The reason was that

George could speak no English and his PM, Sir Robert Walpole, knew no German or French, so they had to fall back on Latin, which neither of them could speak very well. It was because of George's lack of English that the king then ceased to preside at cabinet councils and the custom was discontinued. Had George III presided at the councils during Lord North's government, he might have heard arguments and facts which could have prevented him bringing about the American War of Independence.

George II

. . . son of the imprisoned Sophia Dorothea, was as voracious a womanizer as his father. He had some of his many mistresses provided for him by his understanding wife Caroline.

Apart from this, he kept himself very much to himself. He never toured the country and Londoners even hardly ever caught a glimpse of him.

His main contribution to the economy seems to have been a plan he presented for ploughing up St James's Park in order to plant turnips.

His thirty-three-year reign ended in the lavatory. On the morning of the 25 October 1760, he arose at 6 a.m. and had a drink of chocolate. An hour later, he proceeded to his close-stool, outside which his German valet, ever vigilant, 'hearing a noise louder than the Royal wind' rushed in and found that the king had fallen face-first off the lavatory board, banging his head on the floor. He was dead. It is tempting to speculate whether a few slices of wholewheat toast or a bowl of high-fibre breakfast cereal taken instead of the drinking chocolate might have facilitated a less strained visit to the lavatory and spared him to reign for a few more years, terminating in a more dignified exit from the throne.

George III

. . . stopped his carriage in Windsor Park one day with the hearty cry: 'Ah, *there* he is!' then alighted from the vehicle to cordially shake hands with the branches of an oak tree under the impression that it was the King of Prussia. For the next few minutes, he discussed continental politics with the tree.

He also fancied that he could see Hanover through his telescope from England.

He once talked for sixteen hours without stopping.

On one occasion he told his barber to shave only half his face.

During his madness, Shakespeare's *King Lear* was not played on the English stage out of respect for his condition.

George IV

. . . had two wives – the Roman Catholic widow Maria Fitzherbert, whom he married secretly, and Princess Caroline of Brunswick, whom he married in a drunken stupor.

He treated both abysmally, especially Caroline. She took many lovers, including the Italian Pergami, who fondled her breasts in public.

His behaviour towards Caroline was influenced by the fact that she wore dirty underclothes, washed infrequently and dabbled in black magic. She made wax dolls of her husband, stuck pins in them and left them to melt by the fire.

William IV

. . . was known for his antics as 'Silly Billy'. At a New Year's dance in 1832, he astounded the guests by grabbing hold of an elderly admiral and dancing round the room with him.

He was also known as 'Pineapple Head' for the quite logical reason that his head was shaped like a pineapple.

Another nickname was 'The Sailor King', after his enthusiasm for boats. He once took a squadron of ships out to sea without asking permission or telling anyone, and the government threatened to resign over it.

He had ten illegitimate children by the actress Mrs Dorothea Jordan.

On becoming king, he tried to do away with the coronation ceremony because of the expense. After the cut-price arrangements to which he eventually agreed, it became known as the 'half-crownation'.

In his living room he kept a piece of the mast by the side of which Nelson fell when he was fatally wounded at Trafalgar.

He never allowed guests to drink water at his dining-table. He always drank a full bottle of sherry at dinner.

He appointed as his Inspector of Palaces a man whom he found washing his walls. The man, named Saunders, proved his unsuitability for the position by cutting a Gainsborough in half so that it would fit over a door.

Queen Victoria

. . . wasn't the po-faced old miseryguts we sometimes imagine her to be. Far from not being amused, she had a strongly developed sense of humour. On one occasion, when a theatre manager was obsequiously ushering her to her carriage, walking backwards and holding a candle to light her way, he tripped up and went sprawling on his back, covering himself with hot candle-wax. Queen Victoria erupted into loud peals of laughter and had to lean against the wall for support.

Her first action on returning to the palace after her coronation in 1837 was to wash the dog – Dash, a King Charles spaniel.

When bestowing the Garter on King Victor Emmanuel, who kept offering her one leg then the other in his confusion as to which one it should be placed upon, she laughed so uncontrollably that she nearly dropped it.

She was considered so like her grandfather George III when young that she was nicknamed: 'King George in Petticoats'.

Unlike present-day royalty (well some, at least), she hated polo as she thought it cruel to the horses. Paradoxically, she loved the circus and took every opportunity to attend.

When a man about to be knighted stood quaking outside the door and asked an officer of the court how he should proceed, he was told he should kneel. The man took him at his word and walked across the room on his knees to the astonished Queen Victoria, who became helpless with laughter.

Her blunt and burly Scottish servant John Brown took many verbal liberties with her. On one occasion when he single-handedly lifted the wheels of her carriage out of a Highland ditch, she commented flatteringly on his strength. 'Aye,' he replied, 'and if it were not for the pernicious habit of wanking ma doodle, I'd be a veritable Hercules the noo!'

She danced and rode horses well into her seventies and was a night owl – seldom going to bed before 1 a.m. and often working up till then.

Edward VII

. . . was known as 'Tum Tum' to his intimate friends because of his rotundity, which was brought about by his gannet-like proclivity for ten-course meals. When king, he measured four feet around the waist.

He spoke with a guttural German 'r'.

A fussy dresser, he often changed his clothes up to six times a day. The idiotic habit that some men have of always leaving the bottom button on their waistcoat un-done because it's 'the done thing' stemmed from a fashion set by Edward, who, after his large meals, was simply unable to fasten it.

He enjoyed going out with the London Fire Brigade and once helped to fight a blaze at a music hall in Leicester Square.

He was given to perpetrating childish pranks on guests at Sandringham. He once put a dead seagull into the bed of a drunken friend and live lobsters awaited the unwary on other occasions.

He slept with a string of sherry corks round each leg because someone told him it was a cure for rheumatism.

George V

. . . used the same collar-stud for fifty years.

He had a pet parrot named Charlotte, which he brought in to breakfast perched on his finger. He allowed it to roam around the table dipping its beak into the boiled eggs, butter and other comestibles.

He was an avid stamp-collector and spent many hours poring over his albums.

When he was on tour abroad as a young man, his parents were alarmed to read newspaper reports that he had had his nose tattooed. He had, however, been smelling at a rather large flower and the pollen had stuck to his nose, giving it the semblance of a tattoo.

In 1917, when Britain was at war with Germany, he changed the family name from Saxe-Coburg-Gotha to Windsor. The German Kaiser William commented that he looked forward to seeing a performance of *The Merry Wives of Saxe-Coburg-Gotha*.

Every morning at 9.30 a.m. prompt, he spoke to his sister Victoria on the telephone. One morning, she opened the conversation with 'Good morning, you old fool . . .' The Buckingham Palace operator interrupted her with the words: 'Excuse me, Your Royal Highness, but I have not connected you with His Majesty yet . . .'

Once, to shock a pompous member of his household, he burst into: 'Yes, we have no bananas!'

He caught typhoid in 1891.

As a child, he had once been ordered under the table as punishment for a misdemeanour. Several minutes later, he was told to re-emerge and caused 'fearful consternation' by jumping out in the nude after having taken all his clothes off in order to shock his granny, Queen Victoria.

In 1928, after an operation for a serious illness, he laughed so much at a dirty joke that he burst his stitches.

On his death, it was regretted by all who heard it that the Archbishop of Canterbury had, somewhat tastelessly, commented on the small size of his head.

His wife, Queen Mary, whom he married in 1893, had previously been engaged to his brother the Duke of Clarence, who had died the year before.

Queen Mary, whose real name was May, was an obsessive collector of old scrap for the war effort. On country walks, she would pick up bits of old animal bone and chunks of iron and hand them to her lady-in-waiting. On one forage, she lugged a large rusty iron object home – only to be asked by an irate farmer to return it immediately as it was his only plough.

She was terrified of being kidnapped by the Nazis. Whenever an air-raid warning sounded at Badminton, where she was staying, her servant had standing orders to pack her suitcase with her jewels and tiara in case she had to flee.

Edward VIII

. . . was a dab hand at embroidery and could also crochet, having been taught needlework skills by his mother, Queen Mary. His brother, later George VI, was also similarly skilled.

He was fond of playing the ukelele, though not terribly good at it.

George VI

. . . was, rather unfairly, known as 'Bat Lugs' at naval college on account of his sticky-out ears.

He was so knock-kneed as a child that he was forced to wear splints in an attempt to straighten his legs. When his 'minder', Frederick Finch, allowed him to sleep with them off one night to make the lad more comfortable, he was ordered to appear before King George V. The old king pulled his trousers tightly against his legs, outlining his own knock-knees, and thundered at Finch: 'Look. If the boy grows up to look like me, it will be *your* fault!'

His fellow naval cadets used to kick him for the privilege of being able to say that they had kicked the son of the King of England. They also stuck pins in him to see if he really had blue blood in his veins.

Not surprisingly, he was a shy and retiring person, given to stammering. Once, on a tour of duty abroad as a young naval cadet, he persuaded a fellow cadet who had an uncanny resemblance to him to attend a public function in his place.

Queen Elizabeth II

. . . occupies the throne by virtue of a single vote. In Queen Anne's reign, when the Succession Bill was before Parliament, the voting was so close that a casting vote was given in favour of the House of Hanover. Thus, the crown passed to George I and down to Queen Elizabeth II.

It is thought that she became queen while sitting on top of a tree. On the night her father died, she was in the Treetops Hotel, Kenya, which is built in a large fig tree overlooking a waterhole.

She has a love of deerstalking, often tracking the animal down for hours on end, crawling through the Scottish heather, before shooting the quarry dead.

She was once a car mechanic. When she enrolled as a subaltern in the Auxiliary Territorial Service during the war, she learned how to strip the engines of cars and lorries and was often to be seen crawling from under a vehicle with oily face and hands.

She doesn't have a passport.

Once, when she was a little girl, she was spanked on the bottom by a post office telephone engineer named Mr Albert Tippele for delving inquisitively into his bag of tools.

She is known in her family as 'Lilibet' through her lisping attempts to pronounce her own name when a child.

Among her all-time favourite television shows were *Dad's Army* and *Kojak*.

She has a thrifty nature. Her curtains at Windsor Castle have been patched so many times that it would be hard to discern which is the original material.

To speak personally to the Queen on the telephone at Buckingham Palace, you need a special password before the Palace operators will put you through.

Her husband, Prince Philip, is short-sighted and wears contact lenses. His original family name was Schleswig-Holstein-Sonderburg-Glucksburg, which was changed later to Mountbatten. He is descended from the Emperor Charlemagne and was once sixth in succession to the Greek throne.

Her son Prince Charles was once a dustbinman – it was one of his tasks to empty the school dustbins at Gordonstoun.

Her grandson Prince William once set off the fire alarms at Buckingham Palace and has been known to put footwear down the lavatory.

5

The Entertainers

Wherein we meet Kean, who performed sexual gymnastics in his dressing room and somersaults onstage . . . Cary Grant in women's panties . . . Errol Flynn – kleptomaniac . . . randy Raft . . . the oddest thing that Lanza sang into . . . Hitchcock's cruel pranks . . . and Stan Laurel's sickest joke.

'When we are born, we cry that we are come to this great stage of fools.' *William Shakespeare (King Lear)*

Edmund Kean, *actor*

. . . arguably one of the world's finest-ever thespians, he was one of the theatre's most depraved characters. He had a constant stream of prostitutes to his dressing room in the Drury Lane Theatre, and the intervals between the acts of his Shakespearean performances depended on how long it took for him to copulate.

He sometimes had three women during a single performance and while he engaged in intercourse with one, the other two stood looking on waiting their turn.

As well as prostitutes, he made love to some of his leading ladies while his dresser kept guard.

His mistress, Charlotte Cox, would also pop round to his dressing room during the intervals to service the oversexed actor – then rush back to her box to watch the rest of his onstage performance.

When the intervals between acts were short, it meant that Kean had contracted VD and was unable to fornicate that night.

After attending sedate and boring dinner parties thrown by his wife, he would gallop hell-for-leather on his horse to the brothels on the other side of London.

When he toured the provinces, his reputation preceded him. Howling mobs made references to his notorious affairs with Mrs Cox during the middle of his Shakespearean tragedies, to which Kean would respond by doing somersaults dressed as Othello or Shylock, shouting: 'I may as well practise as it may one day come back to this . . .' (He was a former circus acrobat and only took up acting when he broke both his legs after falling from a horse.)

Like many an actor before and since, he loved to be seen. He could often be viewed reclining in the stern of his rowing boat on the Thames in the company of his pet lion. He also rode his magnificent black stallion, Shylock, up and down the steps of the theatre and he was fond of dressing as a Red Indian chief.

Cary Grant, *screen idol*

. . . experimented regularly with LSD as part of psychotherapy sessions.

He was an acrobat and once appeared on the same bill as George Formby – *Senior*.

One of his first jobs in America was as a gaudily dressed stiltwalker on six-foot stilts advertising the attractions at Coney Island Amusement Park.

He once admitted to wearing women's nylon panties as they were easier to wash and pack.

He has been known to save the buttons off his shirts and the string from parcels to use again.

When staying at the Plaza Hotel in New York, he saw 'English muffins' advertised on the menu and ordered them for breakfast. When only three half-slices were brought to his room instead of four (which would have made two complete muffins – i.e. muffins *plural*) he asked the waiter why this was the case. The waiter shrugged and said he didn't know so Cary went all along the hotel's chain of command trying to find out why he had only received one muffin and a half. Meeting a blank response all the way, he phoned the hotel's owner, Conrad Hilton, who was in Istanbul at the time! At a cost of several hundred dollars on the phone bill, Hilton explained that a hotel efficiency expert had claimed that most people leave the fourth slice of muffin on the plate – because it was too much for them to eat. In which case, replied Cary, the menu should in all fairness to the consumer be altered to read 'a muffin and a half' instead of muffins plural. Which it *was*.

Errol Flynn, *swashbuckler*

. . . led a more colourful life off-screen then he did on it. He was a slave-trader in New Guinea, where he rounded up natives to be sold into bondage as plantation workers. A warrant was issued for his arrest in connection with these illegal activities.

He worked on a sheep farm in Queensland, castrating lambs by biting off their testicles between his teeth.

He was also a kleptomaniac – stealing watches, jewellery, underwear and ornaments from friends. When he died, he had drawers full of stolen property at his home.

When his next-door neighbour, gossip columnist Hedda Hopper, complained about the noise of the rows between Flynn and his wife, he came out and masturbated over her front door.

In his Hollywood home, he had trick chairs which shot out giant penises between the legs of anyone who sat down on them.

His own penis, contrary to popular belief, was only slightly larger than average.

George Raft, *screen tough guy*

. . . worked in his younger days as a truck driver for Prohibition racketeers. His lifelong gangland connections led to him being barred from entering Britain as an undesirable person.

His chief pleasure was sexual intercourse – averaging two women a day for many years, chiefly high-class prostitutes who enjoyed his talents as a lovemaker.

Once, in a single night, he made love to seven beautiful chorus girls one after the other – then slept in a state of exhausted bliss for the next twenty-four hours.

He employed a barber to shave off all his body hair twice a day.

Mario Lanza, *tenor*

. . . who had an indisputably heavenly voice, also believed that he *heard* heavenly voices – namely, that of the dead singer Enrico Caruso (whom Lanza had impersonated in *The Great Caruso*). He claimed that Caruso spoke to him from the grave and gave him advice.

He joined Caruso at the early age of thirty-eight when he died in a Rome hospital in 1959, murdered, claimed one biographer, by the Mafia after refusing to sing at a concert organized by them.

When bikini-wearing actress Inger Stevens asked him to sing for her, he hoisted her up on to a piano, pulled down the bottom half of her bikini, spread her legs and warbled into her private parts. He told her: 'For the first time, Lanza's high note will come out of a woman's body . . .'

Jerry Lee Lewis, *rock star*

. . . nicknamed 'The Killer' by his adoring fans, he originally had plans to become a preacher.

He caused a furore when he married his third cousin Myra when she was only thirteen years old.

John Barrymore, *actor*

. . . had a pet king vulture named Maloney. He fed it on rotten meat, which he obtained by scavenging in his neighbours' dustbins in the early hours of the morning.

Cecil B. De Mille, *film-maker*

. . . had a collection of shrunken heads – over two hundred in all.

He was a foot fetishist – he adored the feet of his young actresses.

Lord Lucan, *missing peer*

. . . had a screen test for a film starring Shirley MacLaine, but failed it because he looked too wooden and too stiff.

W. C. Fields, *screen comedian*

. . . had hundreds of bank accounts throughout America and different parts of the world which he had opened under false names to hide his assets from the taxman. He was even known to alight from trains which were making a temporary stop in a station and rush to the nearest bank to start a new account. When he died in 1946, hundreds of thousands of dollars remained untraced.

Bud Abbott and Lou Costello, *screen comedy double act*

. . . Abbott was an epileptic and at the start of an attack onstage, his partner Costello had to punch him in the stomach to try to shock him out of it. Audiences would laugh, thinking it was all part of the act.

Because of his fear of his distressing ailment, he would drink large amounts of whisky every night to knock himself out.

When unable in later years to pay the income tax he owed, he asked all Abbott and Costello fans to send him 50 cents each to help him out.

Costello refused to work in pictures with Abbott unless he was paid 60 per cent to Abbott's 40 per cent, and used to show his wage slip to workers on the set in order to brag about it.

He used to expropriate studio props that he had taken a fancy to for use in his home.

He wanted the name of the act changed to Costello and Abbott and threatened to walk out if it wasn't. He split up temporarily with his partner in 1945 – all because Abbott had hired a domestic employee whom he had once fired.

Buffalo Bill Cody, *Wild West showman*

. . . should, for the purposes of accuracy, if not romance, have been called 'Bison' Bill. What he actually slaughtered on the plains of the Wild West were not buffalo but bison.

When his attention wandered from his wife Lulu to other women, she tried a drastic remedy. She obtained a love potion called 'Dragon's Blood' from a gypsy and spiked his coffee with large quantities of it. The result was that he collapsed and was unable to speak for some time. When he wised up to what was happening, he switched cups, causing his wife to imbibe the potion, which made her dreadfully sick.

When he died, his fellow Freemasons attended his funeral and his Freemason's apron was dropped into his grave.

Gilbert Harding, *TV panellist*

. . . worked, before the fifties brought him television fame, as a bobby on the beat in Bradford.

He had the rather startling custom of conducting conversations with visitors to his house while lying stark naked in the bath.

Harold Lloyd, *silent film comedy star*

. . . was posing for publicity stills with what he thought was a dummy bomb when it exploded and blew off his right index finger and thumb. In subsequent films, he was obliged to wear a glove, until ace Hollywood make-up man Wally Westmore made him lifelike substitutes for the missing digits.

Buster Keaton, *screen comedy star*

. . . developed his famous deadpan expression from his days as a tiny tot on the vaudeville stage when he was part of a knockabout act with his parents. His father, realizing that the youngster's solemn expression brought the act big laughs, would hit him if he ever attempted to smile.

He was frequently beaten by his father, who was often drunk. On one occasion, to quieten some noisy drunken hecklers, his father picked him up and threw him off the stage at them.

His sex life with his wife Natalie ended abruptly after the intervention of her two sisters, who thought that she had done enough in that direction by providing him with a couple of sons. He was never allowed to make love to her again.

He became an alcoholic and married his second wife, Mae Scribbens, during a drinking binge in Mexico City – and couldn't remember anything about it afterwards.

When he married his third wife, Eleanor, he was twenty-three years older than she was. This so confused the justice officiating at the ceremony that he tried to marry Buster off to the bride's mother.

Bill Tilden, *US tennis star and Wimbledon victor in 1920*

. . . would never take a wash. His clothes were so dirty and his body odour so pronounced that the other star tennis players complained about having to share a dressing room with him.

His mother frightened him away from female company with horror stories of how he would get VD. This had the effect of driving him towards lovers of his own sex. On one notable occasion, when a police patrol car flagged down a vehicle which had been wandering all over the road, they discovered Tilden masturbating the young boy at the wheel.

Alfred Hitchcock, *film director*

. . . once astonished a newspaper reporter who had been sent to interview him over dinner by eating an extra-thick steak followed by an ice-cream, followed by *another* extra-thick steak and ice-cream and then *yet another* extra-thick steak and ice-cream.

His interest in the criminal mind started when, as a young man, he spent whole days at the Old Bailey in London as an eager spectator at murder trials.

While making the film *Marnie*, he became sexually obsessed with Tippi Hendren, the leading lady. After an embarrassing episode in her trailer when she turned down his fumbling and unwelcome advances, he lost all interest in the film.

He was an inveterate prankster. He sent an actress 400 smoked herrings as a birthday present; he gave a dinner-party where all the food was dyed blue; if he borrowed a few pounds from someone on the set, he would return it the next day *all in farthings*; and an actor once returned to his dressing room after filming to find it occupied by a horse.

Perhaps his most dastardly deed was to bet a studio technician that he would not dare spend the night in the dark studio alone. When the man accepted the bet, he had him handcuffed to a camera and then gave him a bottle of brandy with which to while away the hours. The spirit, however, had been laced with a super-laxative and the film crew arrived the next morning to find the distressed technician surrounded by his own excreta.

D. W. Griffith, *silent-film maker*

. . . had a fetish for shoes – owning a large collection of footwear which had once belonged to some of the most beautiful actresses in Hollywood.

Hedy Lamarr, *actress*

. . . claimed that in the film *Ecstasy*, the director, when shooting a scene in which she was supposed to be making love in the nude, stuck a safety pin in her bottom in order to obtain a suitably pained expression reminiscent of orgasm.

Nijinksy, *ballet dancer*

. . . went insane at the age of thirty-one and would stare at the audience instead of dancing – for long periods at a time.

Sir Cedric Hardwicke, *actor*

. . . suffered from impotence and introduced himself, ironically, as Sir Seldom Hardprick.

Marilyn Monroe, *screen goddess*

. . . suffered from Menière's disease – a distressing ailment causing her vertigo, vomiting, and bouts of deafness in one ear.

She was a descendant of James Monroe, the fifth president of the United States.

She was raped at the age of eleven.

She died in 1962 in strange circumstances. Although blood samples taken from her body showed large amounts of drugs in her blood, her stomach showed no traces of the capsules that should have been there – leading to speculation that she had been injected with a lethal dose: i.e. *murdered*.

Maurice Chevalier, *entertainer*

. . . for many people the epitome of Gallic suavity, made his showbusiness début at the age of twelve singing filthy songs to Parisian café crowds, mainly prostitutes and pimps.

Larry Hagman, *actor*

. . . has taken a vow of silence and refuses to speak for one full day a week – usually Sundays.

Hates smoking and will turn his pocket-fan on people who sit next to him in restaurants smoking cigarettes.

His CB handle is 'The Mad Monk of Malibu'.

He has been known to celebrate American Independence Day by heading a parade along the beach in a gorilla skin and banging a drum.

Perry Como, *singer*

. . . was blacklisted in Hollywood for a time after singing 'Happy Birthday' at the studio birthday party of the tyrannical boss of MGM, Louis B. Mayer. His tribute ended with the words 'Happy Birthday, dear L. B., and *fuh . . . uh . . . uck you!*' He became a hero to many of the stars present who all secretly hated Mayer's guts.

Judy Garland, *singer and movie star*

. . . shared the same sad end as King George II of England inasmuch as she died on the lavatory. She was found in that position by her husband Mickey Deans at their house in London in 1969.

Jayne Mansfield, *screen beauty*

. . . was decapitated in a car accident in 1967.

She had sex with Elvis Presley, for which he gave her a pink motor-cycle as a present.

Stan Laurel, *comedian*

. . . was a born practical joker who delighted in madcap pranks with a touch of the bizarre. Once, when dining with invited guests at his Hollywood home, he pretended to choke on a rabbit bone. Retching loudly, he doubled up and vomited all over his plate in front of his horrified friends. They were even more horrified when he started to pick up the contents of the plate on his knife and fork and eat them. Their horror was only slightly abated when he laughingly revealed a hot-water bottle concealed under his jacket, which he had previously filled with cold carrots and peas to resemble sick.

Sometimes, he would throw himself on the floor pretending to have an epileptic fit – made to look all the more realistic by the foam that was issuing from his mouth. In reality, the foam came from two Alka Seltzers secreted under his tongue.

He told friends that he had been given the Christian name Stanley in memory of the British explorer Henry Morton Stanley.

Oliver Hardy, *Stan's partner*

. . . was colour-prejudiced and often told jokes in which coloured people were the butt of the jest. When a band-leader brought a dark-skinned girl to a party he had organized, he picked the man up by the lapels and threw him against a wall.

6
Leaders

Wherein we hear of Boney's part up for auction . . .
Gladstone's whip-round . . . Churchill's Iroquois ancestor . . . Livingstone's reply to that famous question . . .
Kaiser Bill and his neck-stretcher . . . Stalin's way with
babies . . . the Pope who died on the job . . . St Francis of
Assisi's strip act . . . Ivan the Terrible's beauty contest
. . . the nude general . . . and Harvey's queer cure for the
gout.

'Hail to the Chief who in triumph advances!' *Walter Scott
(1771–1832)* ('The Lady of the Lake')

Napoleon Bonaparte, *French emperor*

. . . was English! At least, for eighteen months of his life
he was . . . Born on Corsica in 1769, he was twenty-five
when the islanders, having thrown out the Genoese,
offered sovereignty of the country to King George III of
England. The offer was made by the island's leader,
Pasquale Paoli, whose secretary was Napoleon's father.
The Bonapartes were all on the side of annexation and
the Anglo–Corsican Kingdom came into being from
1794 until 1796, when it became a province of France.

Napoleon was urged by Paoli to accept a commission in the British army, which Napoleon turned down – thus altering the whole history of Europe. After the Battle of Waterloo, he applied to become a British citizen.

He had a morbid fear of cats and refused to enter any room where a cat was present. Once, he was seen lunging wildly at some tapestries with a sabre – the thrusts being directed at a little kitten which had crawled behind them.

He believed that hot baths could cure constipation, from which he constantly suffered and which gave him piles.

He ate his food extremely rapidly (à la Mussolini) and threw balls of bread up in the air to catch in his mouth.

He had a hatred of novels. When he caught a maidservant reading a love story, he snatched it from her and threw it in the fire. His preferred reading was a book of logarithms.

On his and Josephine's wedding night, her pet dog jumped under the blankets and bit him, thinking he was attacking her – when he was simply making love.

Sad to say, for such a great French lover, he is buried without his penis. It was purloined after his post-mortem in 1821 by a priest. In 1971, the withered shrunken member came up for auction in London but was withdrawn from bidding after failing to reach the reserve price.

Horatio Nelson, *admiral*

. . . contrary to the popular image of him, never wore an eye-patch – neither did he lose his eye. He lost the *sight* of his right eye in 1794, but the difference between his bad right eye and his good left one was scarcely noticeable. He wore a green shade attached under the brim of his cocked hat, more to protect his left eye from the glare of the sun on the sea than to hide any slight disfigurement.

He felt self-conscious about the name Horatio and attempted to call himself Horace when he was a youngster, but his Norfolk clergyman father prevented him from doing so.

His life was saved by his coxswain John Sykes at the blockade of Cadiz when Sykes held up his own hand to parry a sword-blow aimed at Nelson – and his hand was severed from his arm.

He died needlessly at the Battle of Trafalgar because of the way he was dressed. He wore a bright uniform with four stars of decoration on his left breast, which made him a sitting target for snipers – but he refused to change into a plainer coat.

To preserve his body on the homeward journey, his hair was cut off and he was pickled in a large cask of brandy, wearing only a shirt.

He lies buried in another man's tomb – a sarcophagus originally made for Cardinal Wolsey. His coffin was made by his ship's carpenter out of a piece of the mainmast of the French flagship *L'Orient*, which was blown up at the Battle of the Nile. The coffin had been made shortly after the battle and Nelson kept it in his cabin behind his chair.

Duke of Wellington, *general*

. . . might have been the victor at Waterloo, but he was a lousy shot in the sporting field. He once put nine pellets in Lord Granville's face, hit a dog, a gamekeeper and a woman putting out her washing. When she cried out that she had been wounded, the woman was put in her place by the general's hostess, Lady Shelley, with the words: 'My good woman, this ought to be the proudest moment of your life. You have had the privilege of being shot by the great Duke of Wellington . . .'

He was a very particular dresser – changing his clothes up to seven times a day. Each time he changed, he rubbed himself with a mixture of vinegar and rose-water.

The name 'Tommy Atkins', meaning the ordinary British soldier, was coined by the duke himself. When a military paper was sent to him requesting a typical name for a British soldier, he suggested the name of a private of the 33rd Foot called Tommy Atkins who had served him valiantly in the past. This eventually became shortened to 'Tommies' in the First World War.

A ladies' man all through his life, he was a sexually active pensioner and was said to be having an affair with a politician's wife in his eighties.

Otto von Bismarck, *Prussian statesman*

. . . was a human medical casebook with all the ailments he endured. In his sixties, he suffered from gout, migraine, gallstones, insomnia, jaundice, 'flu, rheumatism, neuralgia, varicose veins, shingles, severe cramps, chronic indigestion through overeating, and piles.

In a beer saloon, he was just about to have his first drink of the night when he overheard someone insulting the royal family. Incensed, he smashed the glass over the offender's head – but drank the beer out of it first.

William Ewart Gladstone, *prime minister*

. . . practised self-flagellation. Before and after his visits to brothels, ostensibly to rescue fallen women (usually young and attractive ones, it must be noted), he would beat himself with a whip to drive out all the carnal lusts which those nocturnal ramblings aroused in him.

He had a taste for reading pornographic material.

He had the forefinger of his left hand missing. He accidentally shot it off while cleaning a gun.

His sister Helen was an opium addict and a zealous Roman Catholic. She strung together the pages of books written by Protestant luminaries and hung them in her lavatory for people to use as toilet paper.

David Lloyd George, *prime minister*

. . . was extremely clumsy. 'He could never open a window at Number Ten without hurting his fingers,' reported his secretary, A. J. Sylvester.

He was utterly incapable of opening the dining-room door of Number Ten, Downing Street. He would grab hold of the doorknob and turn it the wrong way. After a few frustrating minutes, he would petulantly rattle the doorknob until someone came along to open it for him.

Henry Labouchere, *MP and wit*

. . . was proprietor and founder of the publication *Truth*. When working at his office, he would take out his false teeth and lay them on the desk after eating a hand-held chop. To make them fit better in his mouth, he would then batter them with a ruler.

Winston Churchill, *prime minister*

. . . had Red Indian blood in his veins. His mother Jennie was an American whose great-great grandmother was a full-blooded Iroquois squaw called Meribah. Churchill's own grandmother on his mother's side so resembled a Red Indian that she was known as Sitting Bull.

He was born prematurely shortly after his mother fell while out shooting when she was seven months pregnant.

He was breast-fed by a wet-nurse so that his mother could still do the rounds of society.

At his first school – St George's, Ascot – his report of 1884 bore the headmaster's comment: 'He has no ambition.'

His father Randolph died of syphilis, which eventually affected his brain.

He talked in his early life with a lisp.

He was against giving women the vote, once stating

about the suffragettes: 'We already have enough ignorant voters – we don't want any more . . .'

After his wedding to Clementine, she was amazed to discover that he wore pink silk underwear.

Ho Chi Minh, *Vietnamese revolutionary leader*

. . . worked as a dishwasher in the kitchen of the Carlton Hotel in London.

Jesus Christ

. . . was described in a 'wanted poster' issued by Pontius Pilate as being 'about five feet tall with a hump; dark eyebrows that meet in the middle; a long nose; going bald and a thin beard so that they that see him might be affrighted.'

This was later changed by Christians to a six-feet, blue-eyed, copiously-bearded graceful person with hair 'the colour of unripe hazelnuts'.

David Livingstone, *Scottish explorer*

. . . was greeted, as any schoolboy knows, at Ujiji by Henry Morton Stanley with the immortal words: 'Doctor Livingstone, I presume?' But have you ever wondered what his reply was – and why it was not as widely reported as the question? For the record, it was an amazingly bland: '*Yes, that is my name* . . .'

He had as bizarre an end to his life as anyone could wish for. He was found dead on his knees in an attitude of prayer by the side of his bed in an African native hut, after chronic haemorrhaging brought on by piles.

After his death, in 1873, his insides were removed and replaced with salt. His corpse was then dried out in the sun for several weeks before being carried *1,500 miles* across Africa to be shipped home for a hero's funeral at Westminster Abbey, at which Stanley was one of the pall-bearers.

Henry Morton Stanley, *journalist and explorer*

. . . was really a Welshman by the name of John Rowlands who had been born out of wedlock in Denbigh and put in a workhouse.

He sailed as a cabin-boy to America, where he gained fame and fortune as the *New York Herald*'s ace reporter.

On his famed expedition to find Livingstone, he took along with him such diverse and superfluous items as an enamel bath, an oriental carpet, silver goblets, and bottles of champagne, which he and Livingstone cracked open and drank together to celebrate their meeting.

Kaiser William II, *German ruler, alias 'Kaiser Bill'*

. . . was born with a withered left arm that hung loose in the socket, a neck injury that made his head tilt towards the left and deafness in one ear. He seems to have over-compensated for his disabilities by his arrogance and belligerence, which led to the blood-bath of the First World War (the Kaiser's War, as it was called at the time).

Even at the age of four, he was evincing his hostile tendencies. At the wedding of his uncle the Prince of

Wales (King Edward VII to be), he sank his teeth into the legs of his other uncles, who were wearing kilts.

To correct his neck defect as a child, he was forced to wear a neck-stretching device consisting of a leather bridle connected to an iron bar which went up his back to hold the bridle in place.

When his doctor once told him he had a little cold, he haughtily replied: 'No, it is a *big* cold – everything about me must be *big*.'

He had the sadistic habit of turning his rings round back to front and shaking hands with inferiors with a vice-like grip in order to hurt them.

His favourite party-piece was to imitate the sound of a champagne bottle popping open and being poured into a glass.

He was the grandson of Queen Victoria, who spent the last hours on her deathbed being supported by him in his one good arm.

Joseph Stalin, *Russian leader*

. . . came from a load of old cobblers – his father was a shoemaker and so were his forefathers.

Incredibly, for a man who instigated the deaths of millions of his people, he originally studied to become a priest . . . even though he confessed to a friend at the time that he didn't believe in God.

Standing only 5 feet 4 inches in height, he wore boots with two-inch heels to make himself look taller.

The second and third toes of his left foot were fused together. His left arm was a couple of inches shorter than the right as a result of blood-poisoning when he was a child.

He also had a pockmarked face caused by an attack of smallpox.

He enjoyed practical jokes – such as putting a tomato on the chair of someone about to sit down or slipping salt in the wine of guests at his dinner-parties. (Stalin being who he was, who would dare complain?)

The skills of fatherhood seem to have been above his head. When his five-month-old son Vasily started to bawl in his cradle, Stalin tried to quieten the baby by blowing pipe smoke in its face. When that failed to do the trick, he picked up the howling bundle and put the pipe in the baby's mouth . . .

During the Second World War, to give his troops a boost, he had several Stalin look-alikes touring the front lines – while he stayed safely behind the walls of the Kremlin.

Benito Mussolini, *Italian Fascist leader*

. . . ate like a pig. He bolted all his meals, claiming that no one should spend more than ten minutes a day on eating.

Not surprisingly, this gave him a gastric ulcer, which plagued him all his life, limiting his diet in later years to mainly fruit and a gallon of milk a day.

He abhorred physical contact and abolished handshaking in favour of the Roman salute.

He didn't shun *all* physical contact though – he suffered from VD for many years of his life and, despite his swaggering projected image of a man in the peak of physical perfection, he was prone to long bouts of ill-health.

He gave up wearing a bowler hat when he saw that the only Hollywood stars still wearing them were Laurel and Hardy – his favourite comedians.

Mao Tse-tung, *Chinese Communist leader*

. . . was remembered by his early schoolmates primarily for being excessively sweaty and smelly, due to his habit of going without a bath for days on end. (He believed that cleanliness signified a bourgeois outlook.)

The nickname he took at school was Jun-chih, which means Smooth Fungus.

An avid smoker, on his famous Long March, in the absence of cigarettes, he smoked a variety of vegetable-leaf substitutes – with the result that his teeth turned black.

Sometimes, even as leader of his country, his manners displayed the peasant in him. Once, in the presence of an astonished American diplomat, he turned down the belt of his trousers and proceeded to hunt for fleas.

Adolf Hitler, *dictator*

. . . was once a tramp in Vienna, sleeping rough on park benches. He also tried his hand, unsuccessfully, at begging.

To correct a condition which caused him to fart excessively, his doctor gave him 'anti-gas pills', which he swallowed by the handful. They were slowly poisoning him for they consisted of strychnine and atropine (a highly-lethal alkaloid derived from deadly nightshade). He also took cocaine to ease stomach pain.

He might, ironically, have been part-Jewish. His grandmother worked in a Jewish household and Hitler's father might have been the result of an affair she had with one of the sons.

Vlad the Impaler, *Dracula prototype*

. . . was a fifteenth-century king of Wallachia, now a part of Romania, who derived great pleasure from seeing men, women and children impaled on the sharp end of a wooden stake – usually through the anus, so that the weight of the person bore down and slowly carried the victim down the stake to suffer an excruciatingly painful death.

When some Turkish emissaries failed to remove their fezzes in his presence, he had them nailed to their heads.

He once forced a man to eat his wife's breasts.

Attila, *King of the Huns*

. . . died of a burst artery on his wedding night in the middle of sexual intercourse with his young bride. (For a similar end, see Pope Leo VIII.) His petrified wife lay with Attila stiff inside her, as it were, for almost a day, unable to move, until rescued by some of the dead king's followers.

Genghis Khan, *Mongol leader*

. . . had a link with modern times inasmuch as one of his descendants, Mr Oqir Huyakt, China's last hereditary warlord and a 32nd-generation member of the Khan line, died in July, 1984, at the age of eighty-four. His ashes were placed in the ancestral tomb on the Ordos Plateau in Inner Mongolia. According to Chinese authorities, Mr Huyakt, who had not been as active in devastating great areas of Asia as his illustrious ancestor, was: 'a good Communist'.

John Quincy Adams, *US president*

. . . was fond of skinny-dipping (nude bathing) and every day before the sun rose would slip out of the White House to jump naked into the Potomac river, where he gaily swam for an hour or so before returning to take up his presidential duties.

George Washington, *US president*

. . . had only one tooth in his head when he was elected president. When that disappeared, he had a set of false teeth made from the tusks of a hippopotamus. The top and bottom set were hinged together and opened and snapped shut on springs. As can be imagined, this distorted his lips and gave his face a comical look.

Abraham Lincoln, *US president*

. . . it may surprise you to know, did not believe in the abolition of slavery. He merely wanted to stop slavery extending to other states and did not seek to have it abolished in those states in which it already was established. Indeed, he firmly enforced the Fugitive Slave Law, which made it obligatory to return escaping slaves to the South to face punishment there.

Calvin Coolidge, *US president*

. . . couldn't resist playing tricks on the Secret Service-men whose job it was to guard him. When their attention was distracted, he would jump into the shrubbery and hide near the White House while the panic-stricken guards searched for him – then jump out of the bushes and startle them.

James Garfield, *US president*

. . . though born in a log cabin, was able to write Latin with one hand and Greek with the other – both at the same time.

John F. Kennedy, *US president*

. . . is an angel in the Vatican! In 1939, while spending some time with Polish artist Irene Baruch and her husband, a US diplomat, he posed as model for the painting of an angel floating over Saint Therese. The work of art eventually found its way to the Vatican, where it remains to this day.

Benjamin Franklin, *US writer and statesman*

. . . was a member of the Freemasons and Grand Master of the powerful Nine Sisters Lodge in Paris.

His father was an Englishman – Josiah Franklin – who emigrated to America from the Midlands in 1683.

He had a wax effigy made of himself which was so lifelike that visitors would bow and curtsey to it, thinking it was the great man himself.

He developed a bizarre musical instrument called the armonica. It consisted of thirty-seven different-sized glass balls set on a spindle, which was turned by a treadle worked by the foot. The musician then applied a chalked finger to the rotating balls, which were made wet to produce different notes in the same way that a wine glass filled with water does when you run your finger round the top. The armonica never came into popular use, mainly because it caused fainting fits in those who operated it.

Pope Leo VIII

. . . died while having sexual intercourse, thus sharing the same terminally blissful fate as Attila the Hun. The ironic difference, however, is that Attila expired in the arms of his young wife, whilst the pontiff made way for his successor by cocking his toes on top of a married woman.

Pope Leo X

. . . was a spendthrift who, when he wasn't eating, drinking and entertaining his friends, spent much of the time hunting and going to the opera. To raise money for his extravagances, he advocated the sale of indulgences – which were pieces of paper clearing the purchaser of all previous sin.

He was a trifle unorthodox in his religious beliefs as he denied the existence of God.

Pope John XII

. . . was reputed to have raped female pilgrims and had so many mistresses that he was accused of turning the Basilica of St John Lateran into a brothel.

When he was caught enjoying the attentions of a married woman, her husband battered him so severely that he died of his injuries several days later.

Pope Alexander VI

. . . was the father of the infamous Lucrezia Borgia, with whom he had an incestuous relationship. As a turn-on, he and his daughter liked to watch his horses copulating with the mares.

He once attended a banquet to which fifty prostitutes were invited and during the course of which they crawled naked on their hands and knees picking up roasted chestnuts. He offered prizes for those who could copulate the most times.

Pope Adrian IV

. . . choked to death on a fly. After becoming overheated whilst fulminating against the Emperor Frederick I, he decided to cool off by taking a soothing sup from a fountain. As the water trickled into his open mouth, a large fly entered the papal orifice and stuck in his windpipe. Frantic efforts to remove it proved unsuccessful and he died.

Pope Pius XII

. . . perhaps having heard of the strange manner of death of one of his predecessors, had a fear of flies. Pius, who died in 1958, permanently carried a fly-swatter under his papal robes with which to obliterate any of the winged nuisances that came into his proximity.

He was subject to attacks of the hiccups. Minutes to go before a live Easter broadcast to millions of radio listeners, he started to hiccup violently. All of the usual hiccup cures were applied, including breathing into a paper bag, cold keys down the neck and sudden shocks, before the offending hiccups vanished of their own accord just seconds before he went on the air.

Pope John XXIII

. . . loved to sit in his penthouse flat high up in the Vatican and wistfully watch the everyday activities of ordinary folk, such as hanging out the washing, through a pair of binoculars.

Pope Paul VI

. . . who was elected pope in 1963, wore a hair-shirt, with metal prongs which dug into his flesh, hidden under his robes.

St Francis of Assisi

. . . was a streaker. After getting into trouble for stealing from his father, he was ordered by dad to appear before an ecclesiastical court in Assisi to answer for his crime. When the Bishop of Assisi ordered him to return the stolen cash, Francis stripped off in front of a crowd of astonished fellow-townsmen, threw down his clothes and money and told his father to take the lot. He did – leaving his son starkers in front of the bishop's palace. The horrified bishop rushed up and threw his own cloak around him.

When he took to walking round the town barefoot and in a loincloth with an old beggarman named Albert in tow, the locals thought, not unnaturally, that Francis was a lunatic.

He detested the touch of money. When one of his early followers accepted coins from a kindly soul, he ordered the brother to pick up the money with his lips, take it outside and drop it in the nearest pile of dung.

When he arrived in Rome to see the pope (Innocent III) he was so dishevelled and unshaven that the pope told him jokingly to go and live among the pigs; he took him at his word. He spent the next few days living in a pigsty and arrived for his next audience with the pontiff covered in pig muck.

Whenever he felt sexual urges arising in him, he would whip himself with the cord of his gown, roll in the snow or jump into an ice-filled ditch.

He was the first person ever to show signs of the stigmata – i.e. wounds in the hands, feet and side corresponding to the ones suffered by Christ on the cross.

He stood just over five feet tall and had sticky-out ears.

Giuseppe Garibaldi, *Italian leader*

. . . had one of the shortest-lasting marital relationships on record. For the fifty-two-year-old Italian patriot, married life came to an abrupt end shortly after the completion of the wedding ceremony, when a cousin of his eighteen-year-old bride Giuseppina Raimondi revealed in a handwritten note to Garibaldi what a right little sex-pot his new wife had been. The spiteful cousin – one Major Rovell – was also Giuseppina's lover and had slept with her the night before the wedding. He revealed that she had been the mistress of many men since the age of eleven and, although she had married Garibaldi, she was besotted by someone else. On hearing this, Garibaldi threatened to brain his bride with a chair and called her a whore – then the happy couple separated and never spoke a word to each other again, although he only divorced her twenty years later.

He never slept with his bedroom door locked, following a childhood tragedy in which his sister had been burned to death in a locked bedroom.

He was a member of the Freemasons.

Emperor Bokassa, *deposed president of Central African Republic*

. . . didn't think that eating people was wrong. When a coup in 1979 toppled him from power, corpses with bits missing from them were found in his fridge. It was subsequently disclosed that at his £10 million coronation ceremony, his guests had been, unknowingly, fed human flesh.

He battered to death thirty-nine schoolchildren because they couldn't afford a school uniform.

His name, when translated, means: 'Butcher Boy'.

'Mad' King Ludwig II of Bavaria

. . . seems to have inherited his unstable behaviour from his family. His aunt, the Princess Alexandra, suffered from the delusion that she once swallowed a grand piano made of glass, and could not be persuaded otherwise.

He had a mania for building castles which are today's Bavarian tourist traps. They were erected in a variety of styles from mock-medieval to a copycat version of Versailles. In his bedroom at the castle of Hohenschwangau he had an artificial moon and stars fitted to the ceiling above his bed to give himself the illusion he was sleeping outdoors.

He seems to have been bisexual. He had a suspiciously close relationship with the composer Richard Wagner, to whom he wrote in such florid prose as: 'My adored one for whom I live . . . My saviour . . . My god!'

An intensely shy man, he became a recluse because he detested being stared at by the curious and hated the polite small-talk that is a necessary part of all royal visits. Consequently, when unavoidably forced to attend state dinners, he had banks of flowers put on the table in front of where he was sitting so that no one could see him. The band was ordered to play as loudly as possible so as to make conversation non-existent – thus sparing him from the small-talk he so abhorred.

He would go on imaginary journeys in his riding school, going round and round in circles throughout the night on horseback, until he calculated he had covered the distance between the two towns of his choice.

He invited his favourite horse to dinner and shared several courses with it. In a show of equine ingratitude, the horse – after availing itself of the tasty dishes – indiscriminately smashed up the royal dinner service.

He also had imaginary guests to dinner. Though he dined alone, he had places set for invisible guests such as Madame de Pompadour, to whom he gaily chatted as though she was actually there.

When he attended the theatre, he gave orders that he was to be the only member of the audience.

He went on picnics in the middle of blizzards, believing he was under scorching sun at the time.

He had a favourite hedge, which he would cordially greet on passing, and a tree to which he bowed whenever he went near it.

His servants were obliged to crawl obsequiously to him on all fours and had to communicate with him by scratching out a code on his locked door. He also made his soldiers dance naked together.

He died in 1886 in mysterious circumstances . . . being found drowned with his psychiatrist in the shallow waters of a lake, only five days after being officially declared insane. Suicide . . . or murder . . .?

Louis XIV, *French king*

. . . was born with teeth. His wet-nurses had to be changed frequently because he kept biting and lacerating their tender breasts.

He was inordinately fond of the ballet and took the stage as a ballet dancer at his palace on many occasions until he grew too corpulent to pirouette.

When vandals wrecked his tomb during the French Revolution, someone stole his heart. It later found its way to England, where it was eaten by that man of catholic tastes, William Buckland – the Dean of Westminster.

Peter the Great, *Russian emperor*

. . . was a compulsive handyman and do-it-yourself enthusiast. He was a printer, watch-repairer, carpenter, blacksmith, engineer, gunner, tooth-puller and firework-maker, among his many interests . . .

He came to England and Holland to study shipbuilding – learning the job from the bottom rung of the ladder as a ship's carpenter. He was an extremely able woodworker, and when an old nobleman of his court became infirm, he made him a wheelchair.

He also, like Edward VII, loved to attend fires and would direct operations himself, often throughout the night.

He was a very tall man and had a terrifying habit of rolling his eyes until only the whites could be seen. He was also subject to body spasms and a twitching face. On a visit to a theatre in London, the crowd, not surprisingly, watched him instead of the play and he hid behind his retinue in fright.

He placed a tax on beards to raise money for his treasury. It cost fifty roubles a year to have a beard. Peasants were allowed to have their beards tax-free as long as they stayed in their own villages, but they had to pay one kopek beard tax if they entered or left a strange town. As proof of payment, discs were attached to their beards.

When one of his mistresses was unfaithful to him, he had her head chopped off and pickled in alcohol. He then kept the severed head by the side of his bed. His wife's lover, William Mons, was also beheaded when Peter found out about the affair. His head, too, was pickled and kept by her bed as a warning about her future behaviour.

Ivan the Terrible, *first tsar of Russia*

. . . staged what must have been the forerunner of the beauty contest to find himself a suitable third wife. More than two thousand of the loveliest virgins from all over Russia were gathered together in Alexandrovsk. After giving them the once-over, he whittled them down to a dozen, who were then subjected to the closest scrutiny by his doctors and the women of his court to ensure, among other things, that they were indeed virgins and also that they didn't snore in bed.

The winner was Marfa Sobakin, the daughter of a Novgorod merchant and the runner-up, Evdokiya Subarova, was betrothed to Ivan's son – the Tsarevich Ivan. Father and son and the two beauty contestants had a double marriage towards the end of the year. Like some present-day Miss World winners, Marfa was not to enjoy the fruits of her success. Alarmed no doubt at the thought of being wed to one of the world's cruellest rulers, she went into a speedy decline and died sixteen days later.

Ivan's son followed her in 1581. He made a comment which upset his father, who promptly battered him on the head with an iron-tipped staff and he died four days after.

Nicholas I, *Russian tsar*

. . . gained his first military command exceptionally early in his career – even before he had begun to play with toy soldiers – when he was made a colonel of the Imperial Horse Guards *at the age of four months*.

Catherine the Great, *Russian empress*

. . . was neither Russian, nor called Catherine. Her real name was Sophia and she was born in Stettin, which was formerly in Germany but is now in Poland.

T. E. Lawrence *(of Arabia)*

. . . was a fan of flagellation. He made up a cock and bull story that a rich uncle, through some misdemeanour in Lawrence's past, had ordered him to be birched regularly. To this end, he persuaded a friend to administer beatings over the course of twelve years.

In 1917, when captured by the Turks – against whom he was leading the Arabs – he was beaten and raped by his jailers.

After his daring exploits in Arabia, he anonymously joined the Air Force under the assumed name of J. H. Ross, and later the Tank Corps as a private under the name of T. E. Shaw, which led to speculation that he was the illegitimate son of George Bernard Shaw (who, incidentally, bought him the motor-cycle on which he was eventually killed).

One of his ancestors was Sir Walter Raleigh.

Orde Wingate, *Chindit leader in Second World War*

. . . was frequently to be seen as bare as Adam without his fig-leaf. In Jerusalem, when an important Jewish leader came to his house, he met him at the door stark naked. After a lengthy talk about Zionism, he showed his guest to the door – still in the same state of nudity, and bade him goodnight.

In Khartoum, similarly unattired, he met people in his hotel room – rubbing his body with a brush all the time, which he did instead of bathing.

At one stage, he ate nothing but onions, which, he believed, were all that was necessary to sustain life.

He wore an alarm clock strapped to his wrist when meeting people. When the alarm bell rang, that signified the meeting was at an end.

He had a violent temper. Once, when an interpreter gave an incorrect translation, he knocked him to the ground with a hide whip.

Dick Turpin, *highwayman*

. . . wasn't the romantic rogue that countless stories have made him out to be. He was a mugger who started his career in crime in the grim alleyways of eighteenth-century London.

When he became a butcher in Essex, he obtained the meat from cattle-rustling until obliged to go on the run and hide out in a cave in the middle of Epping Forest.

After a spell of deer-poaching, he joined a vicious band of housebreakers, who, on one occasion when they found little money at a house, roasted an old man several times over an open fire.

In 1737, he murdered a forester who discovered his hide-out in the woods.

Sir Isaac Newton, *scientist*

. . . was so preoccupied with his theories about gravity that it made him shockingly forgetful. Sometimes, he would find himself in the street half-dressed and would run back into the house in embarrassment. When giving dinner to some friends, he left them to get a bottle of wine from the cellar but fell into such deep thought about a problem that he went into his room, put on a surplice and went to chapel.

Once, having dismounted from his horse to lead it up a hill, the animal slipped unnoticed out of its bridle. Newton only discovered it missing when he turned to re-mount it at the top of the hill.

He was a trifle priggish. When a foreign chemist whose skill and knowledge he admired greatly told him a dirty story about a nun, he never associated with the man again.

Diogenes, *Greek philosopher*

. . . on observing in the middle of a discourse he was giving on the subject of virtue that the numbers of the listeners grew less and less, he started to sing a dirty song in a loud voice, which immediately caused a large crowd to gather around him. Said he: 'See how willingly a fool is listened to when a wise man is neglected . . .'

John Wesley, *founder of Methodism*

. . . was the author of a pamphlet on medicine in which he advised the wearing of celandine leaves on the feet as a cure for jaundice. He also advocated the taking of three pounds of mercury, swallowed an ounce at a time, as a remedy for a strangulated hernia.

Bonny Prince Charlie, *Stuart pretender to the English throne*

. . . was a woman-beater and a drunkard. Exiled on the Continent after his defeat in the '45 Rebellion, he turned to the bottle for solace.

He frequently gave his girlfriends thrashings. When he married the nineteen-year-old Princess Louise of Stolberg-Gedern at the age of fifty-one, he continued to drink heavily. In 1780, the drunken prince – who was sleeping apart from his wife – burst into her bedroom and raped her. He was only prevented from killing her by the intervention of servants.

Kublai Khan, *Mongol emperor*

. . . firmly believed that intelligent demons controlled the weather, and employed sorcerers to keep them in good humour and thus spare his palace and himself from the adverse effects of storms and bad weather.

Xerxes, *Persian king*

. . . bestowed kingly retribution on a stretch of water. When a bridge he had erected between Sestos and Abydos was washed away, he ordered the Hellespont to receive three hundred lashes from a whip – and he threw in a pair of iron fetters for good measure.

Oliver Cromwell, *Commonwealth protector*

. . . was so overjoyed after signing the death-warrant of King Charles I that he flicked ink in the face of the man

standing next to him – with the same pen that had just sealed the king's fate.

Alcibiades, *Greek statesman*

. . . cut off the tail of his dog to give his fellow-Athenians something to talk about, on the grounds that they could find worse things to say about him . . .

Charles Lindbergh, *aviator*

. . . enjoyed gruesome practical jokes. These included filling a friend's bed with live snakes, lizards and frogs; stuffing dead polecats into pillows; substituting paraffin for a jug of iced water (resulting in an acquaintance badly burning his throat) and letting loose a skunk in a room filled with fellow air cadets.

A conscientious citizen, he always paid extra income tax in case he had underestimated what he owed.

Christopher Columbus, *Italian navigator*

. . . not only didn't discover America (he was beaten to it by Vikings and Irish monks centuries before or, as Oscar Wilde put it – 'it had often been discovered before but it had always been hushed up . . .'), but when he landed on the American mainland, he thought he had arrived in Asia.

We also have him to thank for spreading syphilis to Europe after his lusty crew contracted it from the ladies of Hispaniola.

He didn't land on 12 October 1492 as the history books tell us – but a day later . . . It was hushed up by the Church as thirteen was thought to be an evil and inauspicious omen.

Columbus wasn't even his real name – it was Christoforo Colombo, but he also called himself Christobal Colon.

Mohammed, *founder of Islamic religion*

. . . used to sweat profusely and strongly. The baths he took to make himself smell sweeter were awaited eagerly by his followers, who would drink his bathwater as a cure for their ailments.

General Charles George Gordon (*Gordon of Khartoum*)

. . . thought he had discovered the true Garden of Eden. On a holiday in the Seychelles, he discovered an abundance of large trees bearing supposedly aphrodisiac fruit, which he reckoned to be the original Forbidden Fruit. When he found out that his native guide's name was *Adam* and that he came from a long line of forebears who also were called Adam, he was doubly convinced.

While on a visit to the Holy Land, he stole bits of the ancient mosaic from the Dome of the Rock Mosque in Jerusalem and sold them as souvenirs.

He was so mean that he sent letters from China on extremely thin rice-paper crammed with almost illegible writing.

In his earlier days at the Royal Military Academy in Woolwich, he suffered loss of rank for hitting a junior cadet over the head with a clothes-brush.

He had an abhorrence for new clothes. When forced by circumstances to buy a new suit and bowler hat for his homecoming from China, he broke them in by tying them in a bundle and towing them behind a steamer along the canal to Shanghai.

He disliked his fame so much that when invited by the Prince of Wales to attend dinner, he refused – asking the amazed equerry to tell the prince that he 'always went to bed at half past nine.'

A deeply religious and mystical man, he had a death-wish, which was granted on the steps of his quarters in Khartoum when, after making no effort to defend himself, he was stabbed to death with spears and beheaded.

Richard 'Beau' Nash, *eighteenth-century self-styled King of Bath*

. . . rode naked through a village on horseback for a wager, and stood outside York Minster wearing nothing but a blanket to win another bet.

He simply adored potatoes, which he ate raw after dinner in place of fruit.

When he died in 1761, his mistress Juliana Popjoy became deranged through grief and vowed never to sleep in a bed again. True to her word, she found a large hollowed-out tree in the countryside near her home town of Bishopstrowe, Wiltshire, and lived in it *for the next seventeen years* . . .

Beau Brummell, *Regency dandy and wit*

. . . once jilted a woman when he found out that she ate cabbage.

Sir Stamford Raffles, *founder of Singapore*

. . . had a bear which he brought up in the nursery with his own children. It attained such a degree of domestication that it ate with the family at the dinner-table and dined on mangosteens and champagne, which it far preferred to any other drink.

Lord Kitchener of Khartoum, *general*

. . . famous for glowering down from posters and frightening young men into enlisting for the First World War, was once a regular French soldier. When spending his holidays with his stepmother at Dinan, he volunteered, on impulse, as a private in the Second Army of the Loire, serving in several engagements in the Franco–Prussian War.

Sir Henry Thompson, *eminent Victorian surgeon*

. . . was obsessed by the number eight. At his home in Wimpole Street, he gave dinner-parties which he described as 'octaves'. He always had *eight* guests served with *eight* courses starting at *eight* o'clock.

Occasionally, there were nine guests . . . his pet cobra was sometimes allowed to put in an appearance at the dinner-table, where it was fed with mice.

Tycho Brahe, *Danish astronomer*

. . . achieved great fame in his chosen field, despite the fact that he firmly believed that Earth was the centre of the universe.

He wore a false nose that was fashioned from gold and silver, and carried a pot of glue about with him to stick it back on when it fell off.

William Harvey, *discoverer of the blood circulation*

. . . had a desperate remedy for his gout. His 'cure' was to sit bare-legged on frosty nights on the roof of his house with his feet submerged in a bucket of cold water until amost dead with the cold – then thaw himself out again in front of a hot stove.

Thales of Miletus, *Ancient Greek scientist*

. . . was the archetypal absent-minded professor. One day, he was taking a walk and his mind was so occupied by a mathematical problem he was working upon that he fell down a well.

Twenty Answers

1   King George V
2   King Charles I
3   Havelock Ellis
4   Sir Winston Churchill
5   King George III
6   They both died on the lavatory
7   Claudius
8   Voltaire
9   Queen Elizabeth I
10 Napoleon
11 Shelley
12 Landseer
13 Swinburne
14 John F. Kennedy
15 David Livingstone
16 Kaiser William II
17 Lewis Carroll
18 Gladstone
19 King George I
20 Marie Stopes

A LITTLE ZIT ON THE SIDE

Jasper Carrott

He's been a delivery boy (the terror of Solihull), a toothpaste salesman (for four hours), a folkie (repertoire – two songs) – and the most unlikely and original comic superstar for years.

Now Jasper Carrott reveals more of the outrageous talent that has taken him from the Boggery to a series of one-man shows that won him ITV's Personality of the Year Award.

Discover the do-it-yourself man, how to become star of Top of the Pops and the Carrott guide to dog-training. Relive the simple pleasures of The Magic Roundabout, Funky Moped and the Mole.

BESTSELLING HUMOUR BOOKS
FROM ARROW

All these books are available from your bookshop or news-agent or you can order them direct. Just tick the titles you require and complete the form below.

☐	THE ASCENT OF RUM DOODLE	W. E. Bowman	£1.75
☐	THE COMPLETE NAFF GUIDE	Bryson, Fitzherbert and Legris	£2.50
☐	SWEET AND SOUR LABRADOR	Jasper Carrott	£1.75
☐	GULLIBLE'S TRAVELS	Billy Connolly	£1.95
☐	THE MALADY LINGERS ON	Les Dawson	£1.25
☐	A. J. WENTWORTH	H. F. Ellis	£1.60
☐	THE CUSTARD STOPS AT HATFIELD	Kenny Everett	£1.75
☐	BUREAUCRATS — HOW TO ANNOY THEM	R. T. Fishall	£1.50
☐	THE ART OF COARSE RUGBY	Michael Green	£1.95
☐	THE ARMCHAIR ANARCHIST'S ALMANAC	Mike Harding	£1.95
☐	CHRISTMAS ALREADY?	Gray Jolliffe	£1.25
☐	THE JUNKET MAN	Christopher Matthew	£1.75
☐	FILSTRUP FLASHES AGAIN	Peter Plant	£1.25
☐	A LEG IN THE WIND	Ralph Steadman	£1.75
☐	TALES FROM A LONG ROOM	Peter Tinniswood	£1.75

Postage

Total

ARROW BOOKS, BOOKSERVICE BY POST, PO BOX 29, DOUGLAS, ISLE OF MAN, BRITISH ISLES

Please enclose a cheque or postal order made out to Arrow Books Ltd for the amount due including 15p per book for postage and packing both for orders within the UK and for overseas orders.

Please print clearly

NAME ....

ADDRESS ....

....

Whilst every effort is made to keep prices down and to keep popular books in print, Arrow Books cannot guarantee that prices will be the same as those advertised here or that the books will be available.